An OPUS Book

CRIME AND CRIMINOLOGY

OPUS General Editors

Keith Thomas
Alan Ryan
Walter Bodmer

OPUS books provide concise, original, and authoritative introductions to a wide range of subjects in the humanities and sciences. They are written by experts for the general reader as well as for students.

Crime and Criminology

A Critical Introduction

NIGEL WALKER

Oxford   New York

OXFORD UNIVERSITY PRESS

1987

Oxford University Press, Walton Street, Oxford OX2 6DP

Oxford New York Toronto
Delhi Bombay Calcutta Madras Karachi
Petaling Jaya Singapore Hong Kong Tokyo
Nairobi Dar es Salaam Cape Town
Melbourne Auckland

and associated companies in
Beirut Berlin Ibadan Nicosia

Oxford is a trade mark of Oxford University Press

First published 1987 as an Oxford University Press paperback
and simultaneously in a hardback edition

British Library Cataloguing in Publication Data
Walker, Nigel, 1917–
Crime and criminology: a critical
introduction. — (An opus book)
1. Crime and criminals 2. Punishment
I. Title II. Series
364 HV6025
ISBN 0-19-219212-4
ISBN 0-19-289193-6 Pbk

Library of Congress Cataloging in Publication Data
Walker, Nigel.
Crime and criminology.
(An OPUS book)
Bibliography: p. Includes index.
1. Crime and criminals. 2. Criminal justice,
Administration of. I. Title. II. Series: OPUS.
HV6025.W35 1987 364 86-31245
ISBN 0-19-219212-4
ISBN 0-19-289193-6 (pbk.)

Set by Colset Private Ltd.
Printed in Great Britain by
The Guernsey Press Co. Ltd.
Guernsey, Channel Islands

To my wife

Preface

This book is about criminology as well as crime. It devotes several chapters to what we know, and how we know, about the sorts of crime which are sufficiently prevalent or serious to cause concern. But when it comes to criminologists' ways of explaining criminal behaviour it is critical and sceptical. Not that I disbelieve the weak statistical associations between law-breaking and such misfortunes as lax child-rearing, relative deprivation, and lack of opportunity for legitimate diversion. They sidestep, however, the feature which all kinds of offence have in common: the breaking of a rule, and a rule of the special kind called the criminal law. As a subject of explanation rule-breaking differs in a crucial way from rule-following. It requires one of the states of mind that make it *possible* for the individual to break the rule. (The importance of the word 'possible' will be made plain in Chapter 5.) Orthodox criminologists pay too little attention to rule-breaking states of mind: hence Chapter 6.

Nevertheless this will serve as a guidebook of sorts for those who want to find their way quickly, through a waste of words, to the findings and fallacies that matter. It will at least bring them within sight of all the totem-poles of criminology, if not close enough to study all the reverent inscriptions and disrespectful graffiti which cover them.

As for law-enforcement, I am not quite as sceptical of its efficacy as most of my colleagues; and I have said why in Chapters 8, 9, and 10. Nobody who has experienced the suspension of law-enforcing agencies can be completely sceptical. The problem is to distinguish what is effective from what is not. At the same time I am critical of the rhetorical claim that there is a genuine 'war against crime' and the assumption that it is one which the professionals can be left to fight. Chapter 16 is an attempt to correct this.

Readers who want to read more about any of the topics on which I touch will find references in the Notes on each chapter or in the Further Reading list at the end of the book. I have tried to avoid citing unobtainable books, but have sometimes had to refer to articles in journals because they present the best evidence or arguments.

Nigel Walker

King's College, Cambridge

Acknowledgements

I have to thank the Trustees of the Leverhulme Trust for an Emeritus Fellowship award to meet the expenses of compiling this book. I am grateful, too, to Dr Allison Morris for penetrating comments on a draft of Chapter 12; and to Mr Hough and Mrs Mayhew of the Home Office for securing the leave of Her Majesty's Stationery Office for the reproduction of their tables from the British Crime Survey in Chapter 15. Butterworths kindly allowed me to reproduce, with revisions, a section of my *Sentencing: Theory, Law and Practice* in this book; and Blackwell allowed me to reproduce, again with revisions, a section of my *Punishment, Danger and Stigma*. My typescript was produced by Mrs Pamela Paige, with her usual uncomplaining efficiency.

Contents

1

Subjects and Objects

The subject-matter of criminology is blurred by shifts of both meaning and focus. A 'crime' used to mean a serious breach of the criminal law, and the Scots and the French still distinguish officially between 'crimes' and mere 'offences'. Nowadays there is a tendency to use 'crime' to stigmatize almost any intentional behaviour of which the speaker disapproves. Calling a rubbish-dump a crime is a conservationist's way of stimulating public protest against something which is deplorable but legal. Calling a legal abortion a crime is an expression of a purely moral view, but with the implication that it should be made illegal.

Within the actual scope of the criminal law, different jurisdictions use different subdivisions. The USA still distinguishes 'felonies' such as murder and robbery from 'misdemeanors' such as public drunkenness and prostitution. England abandoned these terms in 1967, and now classifies offences as 'arrestable'—for which a person can be arrested without a warrant—and 'non-arrestable', for which a warrant for arrest is needed. Some are 'indictable only', and must be tried by a judge and jury; some are 'summary', and are tried by magistrates' courts without a jury; some are 'triable either way', the choice being left sometimes to the defendant, sometimes to the magistrates before whom the defendant makes his first appearance.

i. 'Criminal offences'

The unambiguous, generic term in common and official use is 'criminal offence', which includes any infringement of the criminal law, from murder to riding a bicycle without lights. It distinguishes offences against the criminal law from offences against other codes of conduct, such as those of the armed services, the professions, universities, schools, and—very important—the civil law. All civilized—and some uncivilized—countries recognize a difference between these two kinds of law, although exactly what that difference is has been the subject of argument. Whatever the theory, in practice the important difference is procedural. Proceedings under civil law are instituted by, or on behalf of, persons, companies, or organizations who claim to have suffered from a breach of the civil law, whether that takes the form of a breach of contract, a breach of a duty, or some other form. Prosecutions under the criminal law are instituted by an agency of the state. There are very occasional exceptions in jurisdictions which allow private persons to prosecute for criminal offences, but they are unimportant survivals from times in which private prosecutions were normal. Nowadays the prosecuting agency is usually a public prosecutor's office,[1] but other agencies, such as those responsible for tax-collection, trading standards, or child welfare, may act as prosecutors in defined types of case. In some countries such agencies also have powers to levy 'administrative' penalties, usually fines, in cases which do not seem to them worth the trouble of prosecution.

ii. *Breaches of other codes*

There is no generally accepted term for breaches of codes which are not part of the criminal or civil law. 'Disciplinary offence' can be used to refer to infringements of rules prescribed for the conduct of people of certain occupations or status—civil servants, doctors, soldiers, prisoners. 'Status offence' is used, especially in the USA, to denote behaviour which is an offence only if committed by a juvenile, an alien, or someone else in a special legal category. 'Delinquency' is sometimes used in the same way, to mean behaviour for which juveniles but not adults are punished—whether by parents or by official agencies—but more often its meaning is vaguer: conduct, by a juvenile or an adult, of which people disapprove, but not to the extent of calling it 'a crime' in the moral sense.

iii. *'Deviance'*

The sociologists of the 1930s and 1940s preferred to sound less moralistic, more clinical, and substituted 'pathological' for 'delinquent'. This implied that the actor was suffering from some defect or damage: an implication which in turn became suspect. In the 1950s Lemert borrowed and popularized the term 'deviance'.[2] This had been used by statisticians to refer to variations in quantifiable variables which fell outside certain limits (such as 'the standard error'). A seven-foot man could thus be described as 'deviant' without implying that he should be regarded as some sort of casualty. Sociologists found 'deviance' a convenient term for all sorts of conduct which law-enforcers, psychiatrists, social workers, and moralists regarded as outside the limits of normality: violence, dishonesty, homosexuality, promiscuity, prostitution, drug-abuse, excessive consumption of alcohol, imprudent gambling, or other forms of risk-taking.

They soon realized, however, that the term was not quite as objective as it had seemed at first. Law-enforcers have limits laid down by law; but psychiatrists, moralists, and social workers have only textbooks, religious leaders, and their own private codes to guide them. Increasing acquaintance with the mores of different societies and subgroups within societies led to the recognition that behaviour which is 'off-limits' for large classes of people may be commonplace and accepted amongst other groups. The violent punishment of children by parents, or heavy weekend drinking by men, are endemic in some sections of most societies. The frequency of many kinds of misbehaviour—such as the breaking of speed limits for traffic, or the use of company property for private purposes—is so great that it cannot safely be regarded as deviant even in the statistical sense. In any case sociologists were less interested in statistical frequencies than in the social consequences of being regarded as a deviant person. Deviance must be defined as behaviour which does not conform to standards or expectations. But whose standards or expectations? The use of cannabis would be deviant in the Royal Navy, conformist on a Californian campus. Yet even Californians do not smoke in church. Deviance depends on company and context.

But there is more to it than that. If it is the reactions of certain people in certain contexts which makes conduct 'deviant' in sociologists' language, it is important to recognize that those reactions can be very different in quality. If people react adversely to lying, it is usually with moral disapproval; but addiction to tobacco seldom elicits more than ridicule or pity. Paedophilia provokes disgust or contempt: treachery arouses anger. Qualitative differences between adverse reactions are all-important, because they can determine the actions of the reactors. Paedophiles are ostracized and if possible prosecuted: addicted smokers are not.

It is worth noting that in ordinary discourse these qualitative differences are reflected in the words used to describe them. It is only in sociology that they are lumped indiscriminately together, for example as 'adverse reactions', and used to reify the concept known as 'deviance'. Unlike 'crime', or 'delinquency', it is not a concept or word which is used by the man in the street; and in this case the man in the street is sensible. Deviance is not a single phenomenon, but a miscellany of qualitatively different social reactions.[3]

iv. Criminology

Criminologists need not be 'deviologists': their field is provided and defined by the criminal law. This does not mean that they can afford to ignore behaviour which does not infringe the criminal law. Breaches of other codes often throw an illuminating light on law-breaking. Even behaviour which breaches no code may do so. Bad school records are associated with teenage offences. Gambling can lead to embezzlement. Crimes of violence are often committed by men whose occupations involve legitimized violence: soldiers, bouncers, boxers, football players. Sexual offences, violence, vandalism, and dangerous traffic offences are often found to have been committed by people who are heavy drinkers. Drinking, truancy, and gambling are studied by psychologists, psychiatrists, social workers, and sociologists, independently or in multi-disciplinary teams, for their special purposes. Their findings, if reliable, are of value for criminologists because of their relevance to criminal behaviour; but they should be distinguished from criminology. (So, by the way, should forensic science. For novelists a criminologist is someone whose superior knowledge of toxicology or tobacco ash helps the undereducated policeman to solve murders. In real life, techniques of detection are the field of 'forensic science', although confusion is sometimes created by calling this 'criminalistics'.)

v. Subdivisions

Criminology proper has several objects of study:

(*a*) the 'natural history' of criminal behaviour: what is common or uncommon in this or that society or subgroup; who behaves in this way; in what sorts of places;

(*b*) the explanation of criminal behaviour; why a particular offence was committed, or more often why law-breaking is commoner amongst certain groups of the population, or in certain kinds of district;

(*c*) the consequences and ethics of 'criminalizing' or 'decriminalizing' conduct: that is, legislating so as to make it criminal or non-criminal. Since there is no current name for this field of study it could be called 'nomology', a word used by Bentham;

(*d*) ways of dealing with criminal behaviour, whether official or unofficial; their intended and unintended consequences; their success in achieving intended consequences; the ethical issues involved. Studies of official measures are sometimes called 'penology'—the study of penalties—and there seems to be no harm in extending the meaning of the word to cover the whole of this area;

(*e*) the study of victims of criminal behaviour: the probabilities of their being 'victimized'; the short-term and long-term effects on them; the extent to which their own behaviour led to victimization. The name 'victimology' is now established.

Each of these subdivisions will be the subject of later chapters, although more space will be given to those about which more can be said with confidence.

Perhaps it is inevitable that involvement in one or more of these sorts of study should lead some criminologists to seize a bow of burning gold, and aim their arrows of desire at weak points in the system of law-enforcement or even in the structure of society. They may become penal reformers or social moralists or magistrates. They may sit on parole boards, on boards of prison visitors, or on departmental committees. This is not a sinful, inconsistent, or unprofitable use of their spare time: if they did not do so their places would be taken by people who know less about the subject. Yet it carries risks. In order to exert influence they may over-simplify: an example is the claim that deterrents are ineffective. They may exaggerate the extent or accuracy of 'knowledge' about offenders, as when they say that indecent exposers do not commit more serious sexual offences: quite a number do. They may adopt an extreme view of a complex issue, such as the ethics of detaining offenders for long periods in order to protect the public. The same could be said of doctors, psychiatrists, economists, and military experts; but that does not make it desirable.

2
Laws and Rules

So much for the words and their users. It is the nature and scope
of the criminal law which now need discussion. Its nature can be
understood only when it is compared with societies' other ways of
controlling behaviour.

i. Learning to behave

From birth—or very soon after—we begin to learn not only how
to move our torsos, limbs, and tongues, but also how to behave.
'Behaving', in this context, means more than merely moving them
with efficiency, or the avoidance of falls, scrapes, and other
causes of pain. It means using them in ways approved by parents,
siblings, and other people whose reactions are important to us:
what sociologists call 'significant others'. More kinds of people
become significant as children enlarge their acquaintanceship.
Criticism or approval from relatives, neighbours, playmates,
teachers, and school friends influence their conduct. The media
of entertainment and news present them with heroes, idols, and
villains. They imitate those who please or amuse them, and they
refrain from what seems to elicit retaliation, anger, disgust,
dismay, or ridicule. (A few individuals seem insensitive to these
reactions, but they will be mentioned later, in 5.iii.) At some
age—which varies from family to family and country to country
—they are made aware of 'the law', and in particular the criminal
law. More precisely, they learn that taking or damaging things
which belong to others and harming the bodies of non-members
of their families can mean the intervention of the police: a threat
often used by parents to reinforce their own disapproval. Later,
in adolescence, the laws concerned with sexual activity and traffic
behaviour begin to assume relevance. After that, much depends
on the individual's occupation, or lack of it. In some occupations
he learns a lot of law, in others very little. A professional

driver knows a good deal about traffic law, but very little about licensing law: a barman vice versa. Employers and trade union officials know their labour law; journalists know the law of defamation. Only the police, and lawyers specializing in the criminal law, have a wide and general knowledge of its prohibitions.

There is a difference, of course, between merely learning what the rule is and learning it with feeling. Children and adolescents learn rules with feeling, again with the exception mentioned in 5.iii. The reactions of significant others to their rule-breaking inspires shame, guilt, fear, and self-disgust. Feelings of those kinds can become associated with violence, early sexual acts, blasphemy, the eating of certain foods, the handling of excreta. The feelings may be replaced later by more rational, prudential attitudes to the rules, or may persist throughout life.

The learning of rules begins almost as early as the comprehension of sentences. The child who can understand 'no hitting' or 'don't touch' has grasped a rule. The first rules to be grasped are usually negative. Positive injunctions—for example to wash—come later. If the rule is enforced by fear, or by playing on his anxieties—for instance about parental affection—he will acquire uncomfortable feelings about breaking it. If he is merely persuaded to adopt it by having a reason explained to him, the thought of infringing it will be much less disquieting. Unfortunately some rules are applied before he can understand the reasons for them. It is impossible to explain the rules about defecating to an infant: he can be taught them only by disapproval, reward, and perhaps punishment. The result is much irrational emotion about the bowels in later life.

ii. The rule-following animal

The range and variety of rule-governed behaviour amongst human beings is so great that they could be described as 'the rule-following animal'. The languages in which they communicate with each other are based on rules of meaning and syntax. It is not only language which enables them to collaborate more effectively than most other species: rules of conduct help too. They make people's behaviour more predictable, as well as easier to influence. Keeping promises is something which only human beings

can be expected to do. Games are impossible without rules.
Manners involve rules. Schools, universities, trade unions, clubs,
professions, gangs, and companies need them. So does almost
any kind of social transaction: trade, marriage, greetings, fare-
wells, dating, insulting, applauding.

iii. Rules and natural laws

Yet the importance of rules in dictating human behaviour has
been recognized only by a minority of sociologists and psychologists, and that only recently.[1] Instead, social scientists have
hunted for 'natural laws'. The difference between the two is
crucial. Natural laws are discoverable by men, but cannot be
altered by them. Rules are man-made, and alterable by man.
Natural laws cannot be disobeyed: rules can. Behaviour which
seems contrary to a natural law casts doubt on the accuracy with
which it has been formulated: the apparent exception must be
explained either by reformulating it or by positing the operation
of some other law. Breach of a rule merely raises the question
'Why?'.

   In fact, the search for laws of human behaviour has unearthed
remarkably few. Neurologists have shown how some bodily
movements—such as tics—are determined. Psychologists have
established some laws of perception, memory, and cognition.
Where intentional actions, however, are concerned, laws seem to
be few and far between, and so difficult to formulate precisely
that they are somewhat suspect. Natural laws set limits to what
human beings *can* do: they cannot transcend the laws of motion,
or the conservation of energy. But when it comes to what they
choose to do rules explain far more than do laws of nature.

iv. Ways of rule-following

Rules can be followed in several ways. Literal rule-following
takes place when the actor has been told the rule and acts in
accordance with it because he has it in mind. The child who says
'thank you' when given something in obedience to his mother's
instruction that this is the correct response is following a rule.
Later he is likely to acquire the habit of thanking present-givers,
so that he does so without remembering his mother's instruction.

Yet in some sense he is still obeying the rule, in a way which can be called 'habitual rule-following'. Even if he does not use the phrase 'thank you' but substitutes 'what a nice present' he is still rule-following: a point which illustrates another difference between rules and laws. A rule can usually be followed in a variety of ways. (If it can be followed only by using a set phrase, or a very specific action, it belongs to the special kind of rule which is called a 'ritual'.)

v. Consequences of rule-breaking

So far as adults and adolescents are concerned, many rules have no more influence than force of habit. Others are obeyed simply in the belief that to breach them would make the breaker seem odd, eccentric, or pedantic: colloquial grammar is an example. The rules of etiquette are followed in case we anger, offend, or appear 'uncultured'. Religious people adhere to rituals because otherwise they feel uncomfortable. Some rules, on the other hand, have an obvious rationality to support them. Traffic has to have rules about driving on the left or the right in order to avoid collisions and jams. Pedestrians in crowded passageways or pavements sometimes achieve a similar consensual rule without any legal compulsion. Queuing is another set of rules without any force but that of consensus.

Some rules, however, are obeyed because the consequences of a breach are not merely informal but *prescribed*. The prescription may take a rigid or flexible form. In its rigid form it specifies an automatic consequence: an example is fixed penalties for illegal parking. Flexible prescriptions merely say what *may* be done to the infringer. A medical practitioner who has sexual intercourse with one of his patients may, not must, be removed from the medical register; and even if removal is decided upon it may be only temporary. The death sentence for intentional homicide is an example of a penalty which in some jurisdictions is rigidly prescribed, in others flexibly.

vi. Types of rule

From the point of view of social control, the important differences are between (*a*) formal, promulgated rules, and kinds which can be called 'informal'. The rules of law are formal, and are promulgated in statutes, regulations, notices, and textbooks. The rules of clubs, games, trade unions, and other professional associations can be found in their constitutions or rule-books.

(*b*) prohibitions and injunctions. Formal rules are usually expressed in a form which forbids certain possible ways of behaving in the circumstances. Less often they lay down what should be done: for instance when a society's constitution provides that the treasurer must submit accounts to auditors annually. One of the features of criminal codes is that they consist almost wholly of prohibitions, and seldom say what should be done in a given situation. People must not have sexual intercourse with their parents, children, and certain other close kin: but the law does not of course say with whom they must do this. There are exceptions, but they are rules of a special kind. Procedural rules (see below) sometimes say who should do what when a person is accused of a crime.

(*c*) substantive rules and rules for applying them. Substantive rules are either prohibitions or injunctions, as we have just seen. Rules of application are sometimes called 'constitutive' or 'rules of recognition'. They are required to enable people to be consistent in making up their minds whether an act or omission constitutes a breach of a rule. The criminal law's definitions of offences such as theft, murder, or rape are examples, intended to solve the problems raised by borderline cases. In English law 'a person is guilty of theft if he dishonestly appropriates property belonging to another with the intention of permanently depriving the other of it' (Section 1 of the Theft Act 1968). Thus it is not theft if a book is merely borrowed and not returned by the promised or required date, so long as there was no intention to annex it permanently. Even if there was such an intention it is not theft if the person annexing the book believes—correctly or mistakenly—that he has a right to do so.

(*d*) rules of exemption and rules of excuse. A rule—or a whole code of rules—applies, expressly or by implication, to a class of persons or actions. In the case of English criminal law this class is acts or omissions committed within the jurisdiction of English criminal courts. At the same time, every criminal code includes rules which in effect say that breaches of the substantive prohibitions are not to be treated as such if they are committed by certain subclasses of people. In most criminal codes juveniles under a certain age—10 in England, 8 in Scotland—are exempted in this way.[2] The reasons lie in our beliefs about the unfairness and the undesirable consequences of treating children as law-breakers. Another example is diplomatic immunity from prosecution, the reason for this international convention being the fear that other countries would otherwise use their criminal codes to harry or discredit diplomatic staffs. Whatever the reasons, exempting rules are slightly paradoxical. They do not say that law-breaking by children or diplomats is not law-breaking; nor do they imply that it is always morally excusable, or that nothing should be done about it (parents or social workers are expected to cope with under-age offenders, and delinquent diplomats can be asked to leave the country). All they really say is that their breaches are not to be prosecuted or penalized administratively.

There is one rule of exemption, however, which seems to apply to anyone. If the act or omission—the *actus reus*—was committed in certain states of mind it is treated as excusable. Inadvertence, self-defence, necessity, duress, ignorance or mistake as to the facts, and lawful orders from a superior authority are examples, although lawyers in different jurisdictions have limited the applications of these excuses in various ways. There are a few offences which in English law carry 'strict liability': that is, are treated as non-excusable whatever the state of mind of the accused. An example is the selling of meat unfit for human consumption. The excuse that the seller did not know that it was unfit—for example because it was canned—is so easy to offer and so hard to disprove that to accept it would make the law virtually unenforceable. Even so, English lawyers are unhappy about statutes which create offences of strict liability; they are seen as necessary evils. Courts which are obliged to convict the accused while believing his excuses of ignorance or mistake will usually mitigate the penalty.

Strict liability apart, it is debatable whether the general rule should be treated as one of exemption. The principle is often expressed by saying that guilt in the legal sense requires not only the *actus reus*—the forbidden act or omission—but also *mens rea*: a culpable state of mind. This requirement is often explicit in the statute: for example in the already-quoted definition of theft, which insists both on 'dishonesty' and on 'the intention of permanently depriving' an owner of something. It is not theft if I take your umbrella because I mistake it for my own. The draftsmen of modern English, American, or Commonwealth statutes prefer to phrase the prohibiting rule in such a way as to indicate the state of mind which must accompany the *actus reus*, instead of leaving this to be inferred from a general rule of exemption. But the general principle is much the same; and whether it is treated as an exempting rule or a guide for the definition of offences seems to be little more than a question for draftsmen.

In addition to all these kinds of rule there are

(*e*) penalizing rules. These, as we have seen, may be prescriptive or permissive: they may make certain penalties obligatory, or allow those responsible for the rules to exercise choice. Prescriptive rules do not call for the exercise of any choice, once it is clear that a rule has been breached by an identifiable non-exempt person who has no excuse. If, as in some primitive societies, there is no recognized authority whose task it is to enforce the rules of conduct, it is almost inevitable that the penalizing rules should be prescriptive, since permissive rules would mean that someone must make a choice. When some authority is recognized as administering the rules it is likely that this authority will eventually assume or be granted discretion in the choice of penalty. At some stage that authority may assume unfettered discretion. Seventeenth- and eighteenth-century French judges seem to have been free to invent terrible penalties. In modern jurisdictions, however, discretion is not complete. The rules say what sorts of penalties are permitted: usually, too, how severe they may be. Maxima are laid down for prison sentences, fines, community service; and in some jurisdictions minima as well. If courts seem to be too lenient in their use of their discretion it is always possible to resort again to prescription, as happened in Britain when magistrates failed to disqualify many bad drivers.

(*f*) procedural rules. So far as rule-breaking is concerned, these say what transactions must take place before a person is formally treated as having broken a rule.[3] Western codes of criminal law say that he must be told what he is suspected of having done, and be given a chance to deny it and defend himself in a court: an example of a positive injunction. He must not be adjudged guilty without adequate evidence, and must not be penalized unless adjudged guilty. Some codes include procedural rules dealing with the choice of penalty. In many jurisdictions—though not in Britain—the prosecutor is expected to propose the penalty. The defence is usually given a chance to put mitigating considerations before the court. Even when the statute leaves the court some discretion as to penalty, there may be non-statutory rules which limit this discretion: in England the Court of Appeal provides 'guide-lines' of this sort.

vii. *The criminal law*

In short, the criminal law, of which criminologists study breaches, is a collection of rules of a special kind. They apply to everyone in the relevant jurisdiction: even their rules of exemption do not imply otherwise. The substantive rules consist almost entirely of prohibitions. They are supposed to be known to everyone to whom they apply, however impossible it is to ensure this. Ignorance of the law is not normally an excuse:[4] see 6.i. They include penalizing rules; but most of these are of the flexible kind which allow rather than oblige certain kinds of penalties to be imposed. They also include elaborate procedural rules, some of which are injunctions, chiefly in order to minimize the possibility that people will be mistakenly or unnecessarily penalized.

The criminal law can be altered only with the approval of Parliament.[5] (The occasional cases in which courts have in effect created a new substantive rule by 'finding' it in the unpromulgated 'common law' are nowadays regarded—at least in England—as suspect and unfortunate decisions.) Most disciplinary codes, on the other hand, can be altered by the professional associations concerned, although in some cases they can be challenged in the courts, for example on the grounds that the procedure which they lay down is 'contrary to natural justice'.

This book is concerned only with certain features of criminal codes. Their substantive rules, and their constitutive, procedural, and exempting rules are the province of criminal lawyers, and are within the scope of this study only when they throw light on such questions as 'Should the criminal law be used in an attempt to control this or that sort of behaviour?' Penalizing rules, on the other hand, sometimes called 'penal codes', are interesting because of their assumptions about the possibilities of controlling human behaviour by threats, 'treatment', or incapacitation.

But first we need to see what is known or surmised about the natural history and social geography of law-breaking.

3

Fictions and Figures

What we know or believe about law-breaking is based on five kinds of information: journalism, fiction, biography, statistics, and genuine attempts at 'natural history'.

i. Fiction, journalism, and biography

The fiction of crime deals in the spectacular, the puzzling, or the emotive. Its authors get most of their ideas from reports in the news media, embroidered with gleanings from toxicology, campanology, archaeology, psychology, and parapsychology. A few have associated with people for whom crime is a way of life; but most have not. Since the appeal of their stories usually lies in the ingenuity or brutality of their plots rather than their realism, they tell us more about the minds of authors and readers than about the behaviour of ordinary criminals.

Journalism, on the other hand, should not be dismissed so lightly as a source of information. Some journalists have acquaintances, even friends, with criminal careers. Others get their information from police or criminologists. Naturally, what they publish accentuates the alarming, the picturesque, or the ingenious, and to that extent is unrepresentative of the everyday. But it is realistic in a selective way.

Biographies are valuable, especially if the biographer does not impose his own theories of personality or society. Most biographers have had the advantage of long conversations with their subjects: Edwin Sutherland and Tony Parker are good examples.[1] Their failing was that they made no attempt to compare their subjects' accounts with those of their accomplices, victims, or custodians, so that their offenders are presented as more misunderstood, unlucky, or persecuted than they probably were. Autobiographies usually suffer from the same fault, although those of Douglas Curtis and Jimmy Boyle are examples of fairly objective exceptions.[2]

Better than biography is 'participant observation': the accounts of people who have been closely associated with the activities which they describe. In this way Gerald Mars—an anthropologist—has been able to detail the ways in which dockers pilfer cargoes; and Jason Ditton has exposed 'fiddles' by bakers' delivery men: both worked alongside the men who were their subjects. Margaret Lasswell lived with the family whose petty dishonesties she describes in *Wellington Road*. Laurie Taylor's close association with the notorious John MacVicar enabled him to portray the leisure activities of some of London's more successful robbers and con-men.[3] Participant observation is more objective, on the whole, than the 'observant participation' of autobiographers.

Some offenders, however, are secretive. Paedophiles and rapists sometimes keep diaries, but do not publish memoirs. Terrorists seek publicity, but of an anonymous sort. The most successful murderers are those whose crimes appear to be deaths from natural causes or misadventure.[4] Employees who steal money by manipulating computers or other complex techniques seldom appear in the courts or the newspapers: even when they are detected their employers do not want to alarm their customers. We have hardly any sound information about offences of these kinds, apart from the occasional case history which may or may not be typical.

ii. *Statistics*

In any case, the offender who is the subject of biography, auto-biography, or participant observation is unlikely to be typical of his kind, if only because he welcomes or submits to the publicity. Criminologists in search of the typical must take samples. This is easier said than done. The difficulties of sampling undetected offenders are obvious; but even detected ones present difficulties. Usually they cannot be interviewed until their court appearances are over; and then only if they are convicted. Even so, they are hard to interview unless they get a custodial sentence. Any research worker who has tried to interview offenders who have been fined, or even probationers, knows how often they fail to keep appointments, are out when he calls, and behave in other elusive or evasive ways. The result is that most research which involves interviews with substantial samples has taken them from inmates or ex-inmates of institutions. While inside they are much readier to be interviewed than when at liberty, usually because it relieves their boredom. Yet for most types of offence a custodial sentence is not the usual consequence, being reserved for offenders who have shown themselves unresponsive to lesser penalties. It is only the most serious offences—grave personal violence, rape, armed robbery, drug-trafficking, corruption, blackmail, embezzlement, large-scale fraud, arson, and the like—that more or less ensure a custodial sentence irrespective of the offender's history. So that unless it is one of those types of offence which is being studied, a custodial sample will really be a sample of *persistent* and *easily detected* law-breakers. This may of course be what the researcher wants (see 5.x); but then again it may not.

Where everyday offending is concerned our main source of information is the police. It is the police who record and report the incidents which figure in the *Criminal Statistics, England and Wales*, the FBI's *Uniform Crime Reports*, and so forth. It is the police who file information about detected or suspected offenders. The *Criminal Statistics* tell us how many murders, rapes, burglaries, and other indictable offences are reported each year to the police. They also tell us the sex and age-group of the individuals who were cautioned or prosecuted for indictable offences, and, if they were prosecuted, the outcome. In the case of intentional homicides they tell us a little more: the age and sex of the victims, their relationship to the killer, the apparent motive, and the nature of the weapon.[5] We can discover that in more than half of the cases the killer was a member of the same family as the victim. Stabbing and asphyxiating far outnumbered other methods: shooting was the means in less than 10 per cent of killings (in strong contrast to the USA, for example). Quarrels were responsible for about half the killings: robberies and burglaries for about 10 per cent. For one's chances of being deliberately killed at different ages, see 15.ii.

For similar information about other serious offences researchers have to resort either to police files[6] (for which special permission has to be negotiated) or to 'victim surveys' (about which more will be said in Section iii of this chapter). Even police files, however, have serious shortcomings. They can record only what the police observe or what other people are willing to tell them, and even then they tend to omit what seems unlikely to be useful as evidence in court. What is more, there are whole categories of offences about which their information is meagre or non-existent: computer fraud is an example which has already been cited.

In the case of most non-indictable offences even the published statistics are confined to those which resulted in prosecutions, and do not enumerate those which are reported without resulting in a court appearance. The most important example is traffic offences, which are so numerous that to record and tabulate all the reports of them would call for more manpower than can be spared. It is only about serious traffic offenders—drunk or reckless drivers—that informative files are kept. The same is true of non-indictable sexual offenders, such as indecent exposers or prostitutes of either sex.

There are also categories of offences about which the police have little or no information because the responsibility for detecting and prosecuting them lies with other agencies.[7] It is the Inland Revenue Department which detects and deals with income-tax evasion: the Department of Health and Social Security which handles social security frauds. Local authorities prosecute for several miscellaneous kinds of offences, such as dishonest use of weights and measures, or unhygienic catering. Such prosecutions appear in the *Criminal Statistics*, but the informative files belong to the prosecuting departments. This is one reason why our information about commercial offences is even more meagre than about assaults, robberies, and burglaries.

What neither the police nor any other agency can be expected to record or publish are facts or statistics about offences which are not observed by them and not reported to them. Anyone who uses the roads must have noticed traffic offences of which the police never learn. Not everyone, however, appreciates the extent of unreported offences of other kinds: killings, robberies, burglaries, other sorts of theft, and sexual offences. Until fairly recently criminologists could only speculate about this 'dark figure' and the reason for it.

iii. Victim surveys

In the 1960s researchers in the USA demonstrated the possibility of 'victim surveys'.[8] Instead of interviewing only people who suffered from reported crimes, they sampled whole populations[9] to find out who had been victimized, whether they reported it, and if not why not, with very interesting results. The first British Crime Survey, in 1982, was equally revealing; and the second, in 1984, even more so.

The percentages of offences which victims reported varied widely, from 99 per cent for thefts of cars to 9 per cent for criminal damage to cars which cost less than £20 to repair. Since such percentages are estimates based on a sample, they should not be regarded as exact. But it was possible to distinguish

(a) offences with high reporting-rates: thefts of bicycles, burglaries resulting in loss, criminal damage to homes costing more than £20, robberies, woundings. In most of these cases the explanation of the high reporting-rates must lie in the requirements of insurance policies that offences be reported to the police as a condition of successful claims. In the case of robberies and woundings the rates were somewhat lower, and the explanation may be simpler: the sense of outrage experienced.

(b) offences with low rates: thefts in dwellings, criminal damage to cars, criminal damage to homes costing less than £20, and sexual offences. In most of these cases the reason was that the victim thought that the offence was too trivial, or that the police would not be able to do anything useful (see 14.iii). In the case of sexual offences the explanation was more likely to be anxiety about the embarrassment which might have resulted if the incident had been reported.

There was an intermediate group of offences with reporting-rates which ranged from about 30 per cent to about 50 per cent: attempted burglaries, burglaries resulting in no loss, thefts from cars, common assaults (which usually involve little or no bodily injury) and 'thefts from the person' (which usually means pocket-picking). The explanation may be that such offences sometimes seem serious to the victim, sometimes trivial. Sometimes he or she may see some point in reporting the incident, sometimes not. Some of the victims are covered by insurance policies, sometimes not. Reasons for non-reporting will be discussed in more detail in 14.iii. The point at the moment is that for most sorts of offence the statistics based on reports to the police do not, and cannot be expected to, give anything like an accurate estimate of their frequency.

Even less easy to estimate is the frequency with which offences reported to, or noticed by, the police—or indeed other law-enforcing agencies—go unrecorded. An agency which records an incident as an offence is expected to do something about it; so that if there is any doubt as to whether it amounts to a criminal offence there is a temptation to 'cuff it': that is, not to make a written note of it. Members of the public frequently report thefts of property which turns out to have been simply mislaid, or removed by some friend or relative. In some police forces missing bicycles are not accepted as evidence of a crime if they are found within three or four days. Even minor violence which does not lead to medical treatment may go unrecorded, and especially when it takes place between spouses. Experience teaches the police that many a wife who calls them in to deal with a violent husband wants to have him intimidated on the spot, not brought to court; so that she is likely to retract her statements at any sign of a prosecution. Her complaint will be noted, but not necessarily as a report of a crime. Sometimes what is reported does not make it clear that what has happened satisfies the legal definition of a crime. Is 'a boy in our back garden who says he is looking for his dog' a would-be burglar? Is the broken window-pane connected with his presence? Perhaps so, perhaps not. Even when the police are on the spot they may be unsure that what they are seeing is criminal. Is that man 'drunk and disorderly' or merely drunk and noisy? Again, they may be too busy to note all that is happening. Nobody tries to count the assaults at a riot or a football match.

iv. Self-reporting

A different sort of information comes from the 'self-reporting' surveys, in which samples of populations—usually teenagers—are asked to name the offences, and sometimes other kinds of misbehaviour, which they themselves have committed. This reveals the very large percentages who have, at least once, shoplifted, burgled, vandalized, got drunk, used a prohibited drug, assaulted someone; the considerably smaller percentages who have done these things several times; and the even smaller percentages who have been officially identified as the perpetrators. These studies are valuable so long as their inevitable shortcomings are recognized. It is possible, by assurance of anonymity and skilful use of special techniques of interviewing, to elicit admissions which the respondents would probably not make to parents or even friends; but here too there is a 'dark figure' of offences which are not admitted for various reasons: mistrust of the interviewer, embarrassment (for instance about sexual behaviour), or a deep sense of guilt. Conversely, some respondents—especially young males—may exaggerate their involvement in offences of skill or daring, such as burglary or assault. A striking feature of the literature, too, is the paucity of self-reporting surveys which have sampled adults. Adults seem to be more reticent than teenagers. In the British Crime Survey of 1982 the percentage of adults who admitted offences was too low to be credible.

v. Cause for concern?

How much should these statistical shortcomings worry us?[10] They are not peculiar to law-breaking. Official figures for mental or physical illness, for incomes, for industrial accidents, to name only the obvious examples, are incomplete in similar ways. That does not mean, of course, that we should give up trying to improve them. But a more important argument is that there are limits to the collection of statistics which are dictated not only by what is practicable but also by what is sensible. Is there any point in recording all the minor cuts and bruises which occur every day in factories? Only if they point to a factory in which there is a risk of a serious accident. By the same token, so long as we acknowledge the widespread prevalence of dishonesty, aggressiveness, bad driving, and other forms of rule-breaking, why need it be quantified? Perhaps it is sufficient to be able to count the incidents in which someone has reported the disobedience as serious enough to call for an official response?

What this argument assumes is that the police, or other responsible agency, will get to know about enough incidents of this level of seriousness to prompt them to take action to reduce their frequency. Since direct observation by the police or other agents is much less common than reporting by the public, this involves the assumption that the public can discriminate between what should be reported and what need not. In crude terms, the implication is that unreported law-breaking is of a kind about which the public itself is not concerned enough to make it worth official action.

This hard-headed line of reasoning seems fairly sound where most kinds of law-breaking are concerned. But there are exceptions. The sexual or physical abuse of children, which can inflict lifelong harm, is too often suspected but not reported. Even adult victims of rape often refrain from reporting it, especially when they are related to or acquainted with the man; and the result may be another rape. Unreported pilfering and dishonesty of a petty kind may not matter: but large-scale corruption, computer thefts, and tax evasions seem also to escape official action. Motorists who fail to report reckless driving—unless it results in death, serious injury, or damage to their own cars—contribute to the danger to other road-users. The practical remedy for such exceptions, however, seems to lie not so much in special efforts to detect them as in educating those who could report them to do so. But what is the remedy in countries where murder, torture, corruption, and blackmail are regular practices of the very officers responsible for law-enforcement?

For these and other reasons I have not decorated my next chapter with many statistics. Not only would they be misleading, or at best artificially precise: even if their precision were not artificial it would have little point. It is sufficient to be told that more deaths and serious injuries result from bad driving than from intentional violence: it hardly matters what the exact ratio may be. It is sufficient to know that sexual molestation by strangers is less common than similar offences by relatives, friends, or acquaintances, without quantification. Precise figures or rates are useful when they are part of the findings of well-conducted surveys or experiments and when they support or discredit suppositions about causation, prevention, deterrence, incapacitation, correction, or discrimination. Otherwise the recitation of statistics is merely a display of knowledge which is at best superficial and at worst spurious.

4

Natural History

With all these reservations, it is still possible to make quite a few general statements about the 'natural history' of criminal law-breaking. Attempts to explain it are another matter, and will be reserved for Chapters 5 and 6.

i. Relative frequencies — _Traffic offences_

Traffic offences outnumber every other category, even though we have figures only for cautions and prosecutions. The figures cover not merely illegal parking, speeding, and uninsured or unlicensed driving, but also reckless or negligent actions which lead to more deaths and injuries than do intentional assaults. Even pedestrians who go in fear of being mugged are much more likely to be knocked down by a motor vehicle. This is true even in countries with higher murder-rates than Britain's. Reckless drivers are likely to be young men or heavy drinkers, and are seldom women. Negligent driving seems to be more evenly distributed throughout the motoring population.[1] Convictions for traffic offences—even those involving recklessness or drunkenness—seem to incur less stigma than convictions for other kinds of life-endangering conduct.

ii. Dishonesties _taking / transaction_

Next in frequency are offences of dishonest acquisition. A distinction needs to be drawn between the physical removal of property from the owner's possession ('taking' offences) and offences which are achieved by deceiving the victim or securing his co-operation ('transaction' dishonesties). The former consist of robberies, burglaries, and the miscellaneous kinds of conduct known as 'thefts'. Examples of transaction dishonesties are smuggling, tax-evasion, failure to buy licences for dogs or TV sets, fraudulent offers of goods or services, demands for money under threats of exposure, gifts for improper favours, embezzlement, 'fiddles' by employees. These are committed by people of such varied ages and occupations that hardly any generalizations about them are justifiable. The most that can be said is that most occupations lend themselves to transaction dishonesties of one sort or another; that they are less likely to be reported than taking dishonesties; and that they probably involve greater losses to the victims or the State.

Taking dishonesties seem to be commonest among young males from the families of the less educated, less skilled workers. Teenagers of both sexes, but especially males, are responsible for far more of the cleared-up thefts, burglaries, and robberies than their share of the population would lead one to expect. In statistical terms they are 'over-represented', and the full extent of the over-representation can be seen in Table 12.1. Most of these young males are of low socio-economic status, and below average in educational attainment. In many cases they, or their fathers or brothers, are known to have participated in other taking offences. Their homes are, for the most part, in the less pleasant neighbourhoods of urban areas. They often act with accomplices, but these are usually friends rather than members of 'gangs': organizations which seem to deserve that name are uncommon in most British cities. A few older robbers or burglars seem to belong to what might be called 'group practices'. The more mature and experienced robber or burglar is unlikely to engage in impulsive street muggings or opportunistic burglaries of unreconnoitred premises, and consequently may avoid identification.

iii. Criminal damage

Next in frequency is what is officially called 'criminal damage', but more often 'vandalism' or 'arson'. In seriousness it ranges from bending car aerials or spraying paint on walls to raising fires which cause massive destruction or loss of life. Sometimes it is a planned act of terrorism or revenge, but more often it is prompted by the simple pleasure of destruction. I remember an arsonist whose excuse was that he 'just liked a good blaze'. Again, teenage males are heavily over-represented, and vandalism is commoner in the more dilapidated parts of cities. Graffiti, on the other hand,

are often the work of highly educated youths: I once found, in a
lavatory of Edinburgh University, a pencilled 200-word condemnation of the Vatican's interference in Scottish politics.

iv. *Personal violence* < instrumental / expressive

Much less common—at least in the statistics—are intentional
injuries or killings. An accepted distinction is between 'instrumental' and 'expressive' violence. The former is committed to
achieve some objective beyond the mere infliction of death or
harm, examples being political assassinations, terrorist murders,
the silencing of informers or victims, the enforcement of payments, the subduing of security guards, and the intimidation of
opponents in politics or sport. Expressive violence gives vent to
feelings—the desire for revenge, for sadistic pleasure, for a
demonstration of power or machismo, for the humiliation of an
individual or an ethnic group. Some violence—especially within
families—is the result of irritation, especially on the part of a
parent under stress. More difficult to classify are cases in which
parents are so depressed about the future that they kill their
children and themselves. Whatever the explanation, a great deal
of expressive violence is committed by people who have been
drinking—much less often under the influence of other drugs.
Teenage males, again, are strongly over-represented in the
statistics.

v. *Sexual offences*

So far as official statistics go, sexual offences are much less
numerous than robberies, burglaries, thefts, and even serious
violence; and the same is true of figures obtained by victim
surveys. But since victims of sexual offences are more likely to be
reticent about them than the victims of other sorts of offence, the
relative infrequency of them is probably exaggerated even by
victim surveys. This is especially likely in the case of offences
against children. Respondents in surveys may be asked whether
any member of the family has been sexually victimized, but will
not necessarily have been told by a child who has been. Even if
told, the respondent may not want to talk about it to anyone.

Both kinds of concealment are likely in cases of incest, or incestuous mishandling which does not involve full intercourse. As
with violence, if children become victims it is often at the hands of
family members. Children themselves also experiment sexually
with other children of the same age in ways that are harmless,
even if technically illegal because they are below the age of
consent: it is probably a good thing that early adventures of this
sort are not noticed. It is offences by adults or near-adults against
young children which cause most concern. If the offenders are not
parents, uncles, or older brothers, they are likely to be teachers or
other men with whom the child comes into frequent contact.
Molestation by complete strangers, though often the most
calamitous, is fortunately the least frequent sort of incident.

The exception is indecent exposure ('exhibitionism'), which is
often committed by strangers. Indecent exposers ('flashers') are
usually dismissed as harmless inadequates who do no more than
frighten young girls. This is a rather dangerous generalization,
for two reasons. Sometimes a sexual approach of a more serious
kind is treated as indecent exposure because the victim ran away
before anything else could happen; and if the case does come to
court all that the offender can be charged with is exposing
himself. (This is a good example of the 'undercharging' which
results from the strictness of rules of evidence.) When indecent
exposers are sampled it is found that a substantial minority have
earlier or later convictions for more serious sexual offences. The
best that can be said is that *most* exhibitionists are either boys with
a coarse sense of humour or older males whose sexuality takes this
inadequate but often compulsive form.

What adult women fear for themselves as well as their children
is rape. Yet this too is often not reported by victims. Sometimes
the victim does not want to be questioned, for example in case it is
suggested that her behaviour encouraged the man, or in case her
private life is made public. Sometimes she is threatened with violence if she tells anyone. Sometimes the man is a friend or relative
whom she does not want to see imprisoned: probably the majority
of rapes involve couples who have had some kind of social
contact, long-standing or brief, before the incident.

vi. Prostitution, soliciting, and importuning

Statistics of sexual offences usually exclude those involved in prostitution. The reason may be that the motivation of prostitutes, pimps, and brothel-keepers is mercenary, not sexual. Yet it is sexual desire that creates the demand which they exploit. If we classified other offences by offenders' motives the shooting of judges would be mere contempt of court. But taxonomic arguments are sterile. What is important is that most countries have found it desirable to control male and female prostitution to some extent, whether by outlawing it altogether—in theory at least—licensing it, or forbidding public ways of attracting customers. The objections to it are sometimes moral, sometimes medical, sometimes the exploitation or coercion to which prostitutes are vulnerable, sometimes the nuisances which brothel-keeping and soliciting create for citizens who have no use for them. Most visible are prostitutes who solicit in public: less visible are call-girls, part-time prostitutes with respectable jobs and homes, and the pimps, brothel-keepers, and landlords who make their livings from the earnings of prostitution. The prostitutes themselves are usually young adults with attitudes to sexual behaviour which have been damaged by promiscuous families or exploitative men; but sometimes they are the victims of sheer economic desperation or their own sexuality.

vii. Specialism

Because someone who steals, robs, burgles, or rapes is described as a thief, robber, burglar, or rapist there is a tendency to think of him as specializing in one of those offences. In reality specialism is rather uncommon. A substantial number of burglars and robbers are convicted of burglary or robbery more than once; but the majority are reconvicted—if at all—for other kinds of taking dishonesty. It is thefts which are the most frequent in the criminal records of frauds, forgers, vandals, men of violence and, of course, 'thieves'. There are a few sorts of offender who seem to commit only one sort of offence: an example is the paedophile. A few dishonest offenders confine themselves to one method of dishonest acquisition, such as confidence tricks, long firm frauds,[2] or wage-snatches. Some men can be hired to employ their talent for violence—with convictions as their credentials—in protection rackets, bodyguarding other criminals, or keeping order in casinos or discotheques. Some offenders seem driven to commit a certain kind of offence, such as indecent exposure or joy-riding in other people's cars. The specialist offender is either compulsive or successfully professional.

viii. Professionalism

Professionalism is taken very seriously by police and courts. Although it has not been precisely defined in law it consists of the planning or commission of crime with sufficient skill to make identification or arrest very difficult. Signs of professionalism are good judgement in the choice of targets, ability to recruit competent accomplices, choice of the right equipment, desistance in the face of unforeseen snags, and knowledge of the best way to dispose of illegal gains (or victims).

ix. Prevalence   31%   +   14%

Repeated offending, however, seems to be characteristic of a fairly small minority. Of men born in 1953, nearly a third (31 per cent) had been found guilty of at least one 'standard list' offence[3] in England by the age of 28, but 86 per cent had been found guilty only once.[4] Seventy per cent of all the findings of guilt for this cohort were attributable to 6 per cent of its members—those with six or more to their credit. Yet the fact that nearly one-third had been found guilty at least once is striking, especially when it is realized that this fraction must be supplemented by those who were fortunate enough to be cautioned by police instead of being prosecuted—quite common in the case of petty juvenile offenders—as well as by those who were lucky enough to be acquitted, to say nothing of those who were undetected. The prevalence of court appearances amongst men should not be underestimated. It is sometimes belittled by arguing that most findings of guilt are acquired by juveniles; but the study of the 1953 cohort showed that this is only half true. Fully 56 per cent of those who were found guilty before their twenty-eighth birthdays were first found guilty after their seventeenth birthdays, and 30 per cent after their twentieth birthdays.

x. Recidivism

Consequently, the majority of the men who appear in adults' courts charged with standard list offences are recidivists: that is, have already been found guilty of such offences in the past. If they have entered their twenties the majority is as much as two-thirds. The earlier the age at which a boy is found guilty the more likely he is to be found guilty on some later occasion. Yet most men—two-thirds—are never found guilty, at least of the fairly serious offences on the standard list; and most of the third who are incur only one conviction in their careers. The importance of the last point will become clear when we consider explanations of criminal behaviour. Meanwhile, however, what must not be overlooked are two 'dark figures'. The 'clear-up' rates[5] for most taking and transaction offences are so low that many detected offenders can repeat offences of those kinds without reappearing in court. And many acquisitive offenders can commit a series of such offences without ever appearing in court, even though the probability of getting away with a series is lower than it is for a single offence.[6]

xi. Females

The percentages for girls and women are strikingly low in comparison. Only 6 per cent of the 1953 cohort incurred findings of guilt by the age of 28, and only 1 per cent were found guilty on more than one occasion. These figures slightly exaggerate the difference between male and female prevalences, because female offenders are more likely to escape prosecution, either because of reluctance to report them to the police or because of the preference of the police for letting them off with a caution. Both these factors are usually attributed to 'chivalry', or, more precisely, to men's protective attitudes to women or girls. More often, however, the explanation is that when a woman or girl does commit an offence it is of a kind for which even a man or a boy would be let off with a caution, so long as he had no previous record. Yet even when these allowances are made, there is a wide difference between the prevalence of male and female commission of standard list offences. Part of the explanation seems to lie in men's wider opportunities for various kinds of theft and dishonesty: women and girls are at home for more of the day. When opportunity is more or less equal for the sexes, as it is during shopping expeditions, thefts seem to be more evenly divided between them, although even then allowance should be made for the fact that women's 'shopping mileage' is greater. It has been argued that antisocial behaviour by women merely takes forms which are less likely to be treated by the law as standard list offences: for example, soliciting, neglectful or cruel handling of children, acting as decoys for muggers or look-outs for burglars, committing social security frauds.[7] There can be little doubt, however, that where violence or sexual offences are concerned women are far less often guilty than men; and in general it seems likely that they are more compliant with the law, and probably with rules of other kinds.

xii. Locations

For obvious reasons, most offences are committed in towns by townsmen. It is harder to shop-lift in the countryside. Cities and towns have the attractive and easy targets. Even when crimes take place in rural areas, the offenders usually come from the towns: one of the results of widespread car-ownership. Country-dwellers are not all innocents. They may poach their neighbours' game, burn their hay-ricks, or maim their cattle. Incest is said—though not on much evidence—to be a risk of isolated families, and other sexual offences are not unknown. Young villagers get drunk, fight, misbehave in cars, and vandalize public property. A few join or help political terrorists, especially in border country. Yet on the whole crime is a problem of built-up areas.

xiii. Cultures and subcultures

Some nations seem more violent, drunken, corrupt, or sexually misbehaved than others. Large groups of their populations may be used to fighting, tolerant of heavy drinking, acceptant of the need for bribery, permissive in sexual matters. Regimes may turn a blind eye to the criminal behaviour of their supporters, and especially of the police and the army. Black markets may flourish. Guerillas may make law-enforcement impossible in whole districts. But when certain kinds of law-breaking seem to be endemic in groups of countries with historic links they are attributed to 'cultures' rather than nations. The countries of northern Europe, North America, Australasia, and South Africa share a tolerance of alcohol-abuse which is foreign to Mediterranean civilization. Bribery and nepotism are accepted in some African and Asian cultures as facts of life about which it would be useless to complain.

Even when tolerance of these kinds cannot be ascribed to whole cultures or nations, they can often be observed here and there amongst subgroups. Members of these subgroups may be linked by belonging to an ethnic minority, a religious sect, or an occupation, or by having in common some leisure pursuit or some political objective. Their ways of living and thinking may involve them in the use of prohibited drugs, petty thieving at work, 'blasphemous' statements, riotous demonstrations. Examples in Britain are Rastafarians, dockers, football fan-clubs, Hell's Angels, and the National Front.

But not all such subgroups have names or organizations. Sociologists have used the term 'subculture' for subdivisions of a culture which have values and ways of behaving not shared by the whole culture, and 'contra-culture' for cultures whose values and ways of behaving lead to conflict with society. A subculture or a contra-culture may not be recognized as such (except by sociologists): even those who are members of it are seldom conscious of membership. But there is some form of communication which leads to the similarities between members. They may have come from the same school or the same neighbourhood; they may simply share interests and read the same magazines. Contra-cultures are obviously likely to be in conflict with the law: Rastafarians, drug-users, Mods, skinheads, paedophiles, gypsies, pacifists, anarchists, millenarians, fast-car enthusiasts, bikers, and egg-collectors are all dedicated to objectives or ways of life which almost inevitably infringe some prohibition.

xiv. Social networks and families

Another concept which is useful in describing crime is the anthropologist's 'social network': a collection of people linked not so much by shared values and ways of life—although they may be—as by repeated transactions, meetings, and other forms of communication between individuals.[8] Whether or not 'the City' or 'Wall Street' constitute subcultures, they contain networks of men and women who do business with each other, lunch together, and exchange information. *Mutatis* a few *mutandis* the same is true of people engaged in acquisitive crime, homosexual relationships, drug-use, or political subversion. These networks may or may not have names and organizations—such as the Mafia or the Paedophile Information Exchange. They make it easy for members to find someone who will help them to find a sexual partner, an accomplice for a wage-snatch, a hireable murderer, or a disposer of stolen goods.

Criminal networks include what have been called, rather misleadingly, 'gangs'. This term is nowadays reserved—by sociologists at least—for self-organizing groups of adolescents or adults, each member knowing who the others are, what the name of the gang is, and where its loyalties lie. Adult gangs are rare, and journalists who talk of them are usually referring to criminal networks. The Mafia, the Camorra, and the Triads are not gangs but criminal networks of a highly organized and cohesive kind.

A much commoner kind of criminal network is based on family ties. Familes share values, ways of life, and attitudes to the law. Adolescents and adults who are in the habit of committing acquisitive offences often have brothers or fathers who have done the same. Sisters, mothers, wives, and girl-friends will often help to hide the loot or provide alibis. Violence, too, sometimes 'runs in families'; and the same is occasionally true of prostitution. It is even possible—though not confirmed—that lack of respect for traffic or social security laws is learned in the family.

Some of what has been said in this chapter about the natural history of crime has had obvious implications for the explanation of it. But explaining misbehaviour is a business so complicated by psychological, sociological, and political theories, and by misconceptions about explanation, that the nature of the enterprise requires a whole chapter to itself.

5

Behaviour and Misbehaviour

This chapter is concerned with the theory of explanation when it is applied to misbehaviour. Criminological explainers have paid a lot of attention to methodology—more than most other social scientists—but very little to the logic of their subject; and the result has been fallacies, pseudo-explanations, and spurious 'grand theory'.

i. Explaining by definition

A striking example of a pseudo-explanation is the dictum that 'a major cause of crime is the criminal law itself' (S. Cohen). Those who believe this have resurrected Aristotle's notion of formal cause. He argued that it is of the essence of a statue that it is a representation of something: otherwise it would be merely a piece of shaped stone. If it were not a representation it would not be a statue: being a representation is its 'formal cause'. Cohen and the authors of *The New Criminology* argued that crime is by definition conduct which is prohibited by the criminal law, so that prohibition by the criminal law is the formal cause of crime.[1]

At first sight this medieval way of talking seems harmless. If one wants to make the point that a necessary condition of an action's being a crime is that it should fulfil the definition of a crime—that is, be prohibited by the criminal code—and if one feels that this tautology is made more impressive by using the language of Aristotle and Aquinas, what harm is done? The trouble is that the 'new criminologists' were selling the idea that we should not have misbehaviour—or at least would have less of it—if we had not been so ill-advised as to prohibit it by law. This may be true of a few examples of misbehaviour. Some people find some prohibitions so provoking that they are stimulated to infringe them, as many motor-cyclists did when helmet-wearing was made obligatory. But if the implication is that there would be fewer murders, robberies, rapes, or burglaries if these were taken out of the criminal law, it is so contrary to common sense that the onus of proof lies on those who assert it. No empirical evidence that really supports it has been produced: only an antiquated confusion between definitions and causes.

ii. Scientism

There are more important fallacies to avoid. The most misleading of all is the scientistic assumption. In the 'natural sciences'—physics, astronomy, chemistry, for example—it is usually possible to explain phenomena in terms of 'laws of nature', in such a way that, given all the conditions which are listed as necessary, we see why the occurrence of a phenomenon is certain, or at least extremely probable. Admittedly, one of the necessary conditions is usually 'laboratory conditions': that is, conditions which prevent the interference of variables which are regarded as irrelevant. For example, physicists can explain why water running out through plug-holes rotates clockwise in the northern hemisphere and anti-clockwise in the southern hemisphere: but in practice it can be counted on to do so only if the water is absolutely still, if the plug-hole is not too irregular in shape, and if it can be opened without disturbing the water so that it rotates in the 'wrong' direction.

This does not, of course, discredit the sorts of explanation offered in the natural sciences. The fallacy begins only when it is assumed that all human behaviour—and especially the unruly kind which is called 'misbehaviour'—can be explained in the same way. Some of it can. Human bodies obey the law of gravity. They are as combustible as steak. Damage to their nervous systems produces predictable oddities of movement, as in epilepsy or Parkinson's disease. The fallacy lies in assuming that explanations in terms of natural laws are satisfying when applied to what philosophers call 'actions': that is, movements which are intentional. Actions of which the motivation is fairly simple, such as the legitimate commercial behaviour which economists study, can be explained so far as large percentages of a population are concerned: large enough to allow economists to predict levels of prices and consumption. But substantial numbers of people will spend their money in ways which are not predictable or explicable in economic terms—for example as a result of skilful advertising. Even under laboratory conditions psychologists of behaviour find that their 'laws' are obeyed only by majorities of their subjects, and not by all of them.

iii. Weak associations

As for criminal behaviour, social scientists have managed to demonstrate 'associations' between some common forms of it and some common social variables. For example, having a parent with a criminal record is associated with acquiring a criminal record of one's own, no doubt because a father or mother with a record is likely to communicate a disrespect for law to his or her children. But the association is not as strong as might be expected. In the West-Farrington sample, only 40 per cent of boys with criminal parents became juvenile delinquents.[2] Even when this 40 per cent is compared with the much lower rate (15 per cent) for boys without criminal parents, it is not impressively high. Higher percentages can be achieved only by combining variables, as the Gluecks did in their 'social prediction table'. Boys who scored low on discipline by and affection for their fathers, supervision and affection from their mothers, and family cohesiveness had a 67 per cent probability of becoming delinquent.[3] But one in three of them did not.

Nor are the associations more impressive if factors outside the home are studied. Low socio-economic status, unemployment, bad housing, poverty, and delinquent companions are all to some extent associated statistically with common kinds of law-breaking; but the associations seldom amount even to a crude majority.

Constitutional factors are no more impressive as determinants. Low intelligence is weakly associated with stealing and sexual offences. Some mental disorders, such as schizophrenia, are weakly associated with personal violence. (Violence is more strongly associated with some forms of 'psychopathy' or 'personality disorder', but since it is the violence that is usually the basis of the diagnosis this scarcely amounts to an association.) Some children seem more insensitive than their siblings to the disapproval, anger, dismay, or ridicule of those from whom they are supposed to learn the rules of behaviour (see 2.i). The XYY chromosome is said to be associated with violence and sexual offending; but it is also associated with below-average intelligence and above-average height—two factors which make men slightly more likely to resort to violence to win arguments or women. In any case, the great majority of men with this chromosomal defect seem to lead law-abiding lives. There is some empirical support for an association between criminal behaviour and an undefined 'genetic predisposition'. The evidence is based on studies of identical twins and of children separated at early ages from their criminal parents;[4] but again the associations are weak.

iv. Sufficient and necessary conditions

The weakness of all these associations does not mean that they tell us nothing. It is due to one or both of two things. First, we are seldom able to count or measure what we really want to: usually we have to be content with counting or measuring something which is assumed to be closely associated with it, just as the police use breathalysers not because the state of a person's breath is criminal but because it is associated with the degree of intoxication. When social scientists wanted to estimate how many individuals in a sample had unsatisfactory upbringings they used to count 'broken homes'. Today they ask less crude questions—as the Gluecks did—but get only a little closer to the quality of childrearing. The easier something is to quantify the less likely it is to be what the social scientist really wants to be measuring.

That is only one reason why associations are weak. The other is even more important. Associations seldom point to *sufficient* conditions: usually only to *necessary* conditions. In the language of logic, a set of sufficient conditions is a combination of conditions which guarantees the occurrence of what has to be explained. When what has to be explained is an intentional human action there is always more than one set of sufficient conditions. If there is a condition which appears in every set, it is a 'necessary' condition. For example there are many sets of sufficient conditions for suicides,[5] since they are motivated in different ways. Only three conditions are necessary: the intention, the means, and the knowledge of how to use the means. (Necessary conditions are often as obvious as this.) What social scientists are usually talking about when they explain suicides are the non-necessary conditions. But if one necessary condition is unfulfilled, no amount of non-necessary conditions will result in suicide. Just how varied the non-necessary conditions of law-breaking are will become clear in the next chapter, where rule-breaking states of mind are described. Meanwhile other points about explanation have to be made.

v. Inverting the problem

One is about an artificial worry that plagues both positivists and anti-positivists. Should we be trying to explain behaviour which infringes or behaviour which conforms? The traditional answer is 'behaviour which infringes'; but there is something to be said for turning the problem upside down. At least this does not assume that everyone is born a conformist. Already in Chapter 2 it has been emphasized that children have to learn rules: they are not born knowing them, nor do they obey them as soon as they grasp them. Learning the rules, from parents, significant others (see 2.i), books, television, public notices, and other sources is a process which begins early but continues, off and on, for most of one's active life. 'Control' or 'containment' theorists therefore concentrate on the expedients by which cultures or subcultures control conduct, and explain misconduct as the result of expedients which are faulty or unthoroughly applied, so that some individuals slip through. (They also recognize, however, that some individuals are, for congenital or other reasons, abnormally unresponsive to normal expedients of socialization.) There seem to be a great many failures of one kind or another, especially where the laws of property, traffic, and sexual behaviour are concerned. Control theory therefore posits the need for intimidation (by deterrents: see Chapter 9) and prevention (see Chapter 6), although these too may fail. This is not an admission of weakness: just realism.

Realistic as it seems, the 'inverse' approach is not accepted by all explainers. Some find their explanations in the shortcomings of their societies, and particularly in inequalities of ownership, access to opportunities for satisfying natural needs, or political power. They emphasize the fact that most of the acquisitive offenders who can be identified come from disadvantaged groups, although at the same time they recognize the prevalence of dishonest practices amongst the more fortunate. Public disorders are attributed to the ineffectiveness of legitimate ways of trying to achieve political objectives. There are types of misbehaviour which do not fit very well into such theories: bad driving, sexual molestation, and fights between football fans are instances. But it is not a fair objection to 'political' explanations, or to any sort of explanation, to point out that it does not account for every sort of misbehaviour: that would fall into the fallacy of 'grand theory', which is discussed in 6.xiv.

The solution to the apparent dilemma is obvious and unexciting. Which approach one should adopt depends simply on the state of knowledge of the person who asks 'Why . . .?': on how much he knows about the processes which lead to conformity. If he is ignorant about them, the explanation must begin, as Chapter 2 began, with those processes. If he knows a lot about them, it can concentrate on the failures of these processes, and on ways in which people may escape them. Inverting the problem does not change its essential features.

vi. *The questioner's need to know*

It is not only the questioner's state of knowledge, however, that affects the answer to the question 'Why . . .?'. His reasons for asking it also make an important difference. There are three possibilities:

(*a*) he may want to find some way of making the behaviour less frequent, or of identifying those likely to indulge in it, so that they can be controlled or incapacitated. In social as in technological affairs the aim of explanations is often to prevent, predict, or produce. Thus if what the questioner wants are ideas for reducing the incidence of thefts it may well be relevant—and not entirely misleading—to tell him that some people steal because they are destitute. Alleviating destitution will probably achieve some reduction of thefts. The same is true of the more sophisticated notion of 'relative deprivation'.[6] For brevity, I shall call such questioners 'preventers'.

(*b*) the questioner may, however, be a 'blamer': he may want to decide how much blame to apportion for a specific piece of misbehaviour by an identified person. This is often what is required by sentencers, by priests who are hearing confessions, or by ordinary people when gossiping about each other's peccadilloes. The kind of explanation which is appropriate needs special discussion in the light of points to be made later. All that can be said here is that it will by no means always take the same form as one that would be appropriate for a preventer.

(*c*) the questioner may be a 'wonderer', actuated by simple curiosity, without feeling in any way called on to predict, prevent, produce, or assign blame for the action. This is more likely when the action is counter to a rule or expectation than when it is of a conforming kind. It is only professional sociologists, psychologists, or anthropologists who spend their time wondering why people regularly get married, have children, seek secure employment, or obey the law. For most people, curiosity is the product of surprise, and in social life only the very sophisticated are surprised by what is usual. In another book I have suggested that surprise is a better criterion of 'deviance' than the others which have been suggested.[7] Where misbehaviour is concerned, surprise and curiosity are natural.

A preventer, a blamer, and a wonderer may accept different sorts of answer to the question 'Why . . .?' Faced with the problem of the unauthorized taking of cars, a preventer might well be content with being told that a great many cars which are left parked for long periods are easy to drive away without keys. Although this is only one non-necessary condition for the offence, it seems the easiest to attack, by persuading manufacturers and owners to make their cars less vulnerable. On the other hand, this condition would be of little interest to a court, which would simply take it for granted. The court would be interested in the state of mind of the person who had taken the car. Did he think he had the owner's permission, or that he would have been given it had he asked? Did he intend to steal it or merely to borrow it? Did he borrow it for some good reason, such as taking a badly injured person to hospital? Had he taken cars before; and if so what reasons had he given?

A wonderer would not be totally uninterested in non-necessary conditions. He would want to know whether this person took cars only when drunk, or in the company of others; how he knew which cars were easy to take; whether car-taking was acceptable behaviour amongst his peers. If he had previous convictions for the same sort of offence, how had the court dealt with him, and why had that not prevented him from doing it again?

At the same time, there are objective criteria which all explanations must satisfy. They must not, for example, be tautologies, as when crime is explained as the result of including conduct in the criminal law (see 5.i). Nor should they be so vague and protean—like Dollard and Miller's explanation of aggression (see 6.xiv)—that they cannot be subjected to empirical falsification. They must, however, take into account, and cater for, the extent of the questioner's ignorance and the purpose for which he wants the explanation. And they must also take into account something subtler.

vii. *Single actions and frequencies*

It is not only the reasons for wanting explanations that differ: questioners may want different things to be explained even when they appear to be asking about the same sort of behaviour. Whether the questioner is a preventer, a blamer, or a wonderer, his question may be about an individual or about a class of individuals. He may want to know what can be done to reduce shoplifting by Mrs Jones, or shop-lifting by urban housewives. He may want to know why the Irish resort to political violence more often than the Danes, or why an individual Irishman committed murder. He may want to decide whether Mrs Jones is more culpable than Mrs Smith, or—though less sensibly—whether housewives exposed to the temptations of supermarkets are less blameworthy than men who pilfer at work. He may be curious about what made Mr Jones a child-molester, or about the reason why child-molesting is more frequent in Hull than in

Huddersfield (supposing this to be the case). As we shall see, an explanation of an individual's behaviour will sometimes be unacceptable when group frequencies are the subject of the question.

viii. Frequencies and explanations

In passing, however, it is worth noting how often a frequency statement is offered—and accepted—as if it were an explanation. An act of violence is sometimes explained by saying that the actor was drunk or, worse still, psychopathic, the underlying implication being that drunks and psychopaths are often violent. In the case of the psychopath, as we have already seen, the explanation is often superficial, since it is probably his acts of violence which are the basis for the 'diagnosis'. Even in the case of drunkenness, however, which is often mentioned because of its known association with violence, this association by itself is hardly an explanation. It is true that for a preventer it is relevant to be told that the aggressor was drunk, since this may suggest ways of making it less likely that he will commit another assault. But for a blamer or a wonderer it is—or should be—only the beginning of an explanation. What passed through the man's intoxicated mind? Did he fancy that he had been insulted? Was he merely showing his physical superiority? Had he a grudge against his victim? Frequency statements can do little more than narrow the search for a satisfactory explanation. They may even lead the search in the wrong direction. Since members of the IRA frequently kill, a killing by a known IRA member is likely to be labelled 'political' or 'sectarian' without anyone's asking whether the man had a more personal grudge against his victim, or whether he simply enjoyed killing.

ix. 'Probability explanations' and 'possibility explanations'

It is not only the requirements of the questioner that vary. The sort of answer which he is prepared to accept may take one of two forms, although this too is hardly ever recognized. It is commonly supposed that an explanation must be in some degree deterministic: that it must tell us that, given the circumstances, the actors could hardly be expected to act otherwise. Since actors in the given circumstances do sometimes act otherwise explanations of this sort are hardly ever rigidly deterministic. Instead they say that 'given X, Y etc. the *explicandum* is probable' (or perhaps 'highly probable'). A convenient term for them is 'probability explanations'.

Many people are not aware that there is another kind; and most of those who are aware prefer to ignore it. In the 1950s W. H. Dray pointed out that historians deal in what he called 'narrative explanations'. In *Laws and Explanations in History* (1957) he gives a striking example. At a baseball game in British Columbia the radio commentator told listeners that a long fly ball to centre field was going to land high up on the twenty-foot-high fence. In the next breath he told them that the centre fielder had managed to catch it. What every listener wanted to know was how he could possibly have caught it. (The explanation was that the ball had fallen so close to the scorer's platform that the fielder had managed to run up the scorer's ladder.) Dray's point was that the audience did not want to be told why the catch was inevitable or probable: simply how it was possible. Historians, he argued, are often[8] content with answers to the question 'How was that possible?'

It is not only historians who deal in 'possibility explanations'. In everyday life we are constantly doing so. 'How could you forget the tickets?' is answered by 'I got a worrying telephone call just as I was getting ready'. The answer does not claim—nor is it expected to—that this made the forgetting inevitable or highly probable: merely understandable, or in other words psychologically possible. Similarly, when a rule is broken the question is usually 'How could you (be rude to a guest)?' A possibility explanation is usually enough.

x. Series and frequencies

The situation is different when the questioner implies that the action is one of a series. 'Why do you always (or so often) forget the tickets (or insult our guests)?' A simple possibility explanation, in terms of what happened on a particular occasion, is not enough. The questioner wants to know why you are more likely to do so than other people; or, more precisely still, than other people of your sort (that is, of your age, social class, occupation, or whatever other category the questioner has in mind). The *explicandum*—the phenomenon for which an explanation is being demanded—is not an incident but a frequency. The frequency is usually an individual's frequency; but it may be a category frequency. 'Why do young men get drunk?' or 'Why do football fans fight each other?'

In practice, where rule-breaking is concerned, the frequency to be explained is never high enough to justify us in saying 'always', or even 'nearly always'. Whatever the rule there are very few people who break it at every opportunity. At most, the *explicandum* is a frequency that is high in comparison with the frequency observable in other individuals or groups.

xi. Are possibility explanations respectable?

The logical difference between possibility and probability explanations is seldom recognized. Roughly speaking, the former is required only to tell us why it is not surprising that something happened; the latter why it would have been surprising if it had *not* happened. Sometimes a probability answer is given when all that the questioner is asking for is a possibility explanation. 'I always insult my guests when I am drunk' is a proper answer to the question 'How could you?' But the converse is not true. 'Why do you always (or so often) insult your guests?' I may reply, 'Well, what happened this time was this . . .': but that is not what the questioner is asking to be told.

A possibility explanation is likely to be dismissed as something that may be acceptable in everyday life but is not respectable in psychological or sociological discourse. It is not 'scientific'. That can be granted, since scientific discourse usually consist of statements about probabilities, if not inevitabilities. That being so, however, it must also be granted that innumerable social incidents which lead to blame or surprise are not capable of a scientific explanation, because they do not seem to be examples of an individual or group frequency. All that can be expected is a possibility explanation in terms of what happened at the time.

The point is of crucial importance when explanations of criminal offences are being demanded. If the questioner is simply curious about a particular incident, and has no reason to believe that it is part of a series, he cannot logically insist on a probability explanation. He must listen to a possibility explanation which simply tells the story of what happened. He may, of course, disbelieve it; and he is entitled to ask 'Was that the only occasion when Jones behaved like that?' If the answer is that Jones has done likewise on other occasions, the questioner is entitled to ask whether there is not some factor at work which makes him likely to do it, and what that is. If the answer is in effect 'Yes', he can then ask for a scientific, probability explanation.

Suppose on the other hand that the questioner is not a mere wonderer, but wants to know how much to blame Jones for a theft. The first thing he must listen to is the story of how Jones came to commit that particular theft. (He may, of course, have reason to disbelieve it, especially if he has heard it before, and especially if he has heard it before from Jones: but if it is believed it is the most relevant sort of explanation.) Or he may be told that Jones is a 'compulsive' shop-lifter: that is, has overwhelming urges to steal from shops. That would be a probability explanation which could be accepted instead of a possibility one, and would be relevant to culpability. By contrast, it would be barely relevant to tell him that Jones belongs to a school which has a lot of shop-lifting pupils. That too would be a probability explanation, but not of a kind that has much bearing on Jones's culpability.

It might on the other hand be extremely relevant if the questioner is a shopkeeper who wants ideas for reducing his losses from theft. (He could write to the school, ban its pupils from his shop, or put up a notice about the number of pupils prosecuted.) If the questioner's aim is reductive, possibility explanations are of little interest to him.

More will be said in later chapters about the use of explanations by sentencers in order to assess culpability or choose a method of disposal which will reduce the frequency of offending. Meanwhile we are concerned with the questioner whose interest is simple curiosity. He must first accept that if he wants more than a possibility explanation for any sort of rule-breaking he must first be fairly sure that it is a genuine example of a breach that is being committed with unusual frequency either by a specified individual or by a defined category of individuals. Otherwise he may have to be content with the sort of narrative explanations which are so common in biographies, autobiographies, and case histories.

The distinction between probability and possibility explanations is sometimes misunderstood as a distinction between actions that are determined and those that are not. In fact all it does is to emphasize that, to whatever degree human actions are determined, in everyday life we usually have to be content with an explanation of the kind that merely reduces our surprise at the action. But this is not a case in which the way in which we explain in everyday life is inferior to the way in which we should be explaining. Possibility explanations are all that it is sensible to ask for unless we know that the sort of action about which we are asking is frequent, either in an individual's history or amongst a definable group of individuals. Only then is it logical to insist that the answer tell us why it would be surprising if the action had *not* taken place. And even then we must not expect the answer to show that the action was inevitable. It may or may not have been; but there is no possibility of demonstrating this.

6

Rule-Breaking and Rationality

Since what interests the criminological wonderer is not why people obey rules but why they break them, his first question should be 'How are breaches of rules psychologically possible?' More specifically, in the case of infringements of the criminal law, what are the states of mind of people who act contrary to rules which have been formally promulgated, publicly enforced, and backed by explicit penalties for non-compliance? Only *when* he understands those states of mind, and *if* he can point to abnormal frequencies of non-compliance in an individual or a definable group, does it make sense to ask 'Why, in that (or those) case(s) are such states of mind likely to occur?': in other words, to ask for a probability explanation. Yet the sort of scientism which deals in quantitative correlations has had such a grip on both psychological and sociological criminologists that remarkably few have paid much attention to states of mind. Apart from those few[1] they have been left to biographers and autobiographers. Hence this chapter.

i. Ignorance of the rule

For example, ignorance of a rule is obviously likely to lead to a breach of it. Infants take each other's toys in ignorance of the laws of property. Adults too infringe prohibitions or injunctions of which they are unaware: for example by locking a fire exit in a public building. Interestingly, ignorance of the law is not accepted as an excuse in most criminal codes, but only because it is too easy to fake.[2] In practice, a court which is thus obliged to convict a transgressor may, if it believes in his ignorance, deal with him very leniently: an example of the relevance of possibility explanations for blamers.

ii. Failure to apply the rule

More interesting are people who know the rule but breach it because they fail to see a situation as being one to which it applies: or more precisely as being one to which most other people would apply it. Men who know that assault is an offence may not see this as applying to the way they treat their wives or children. People in positions of power who accept gifts are surprised when accused of corruption. Rugby players whose celebrations cause damage to property do not see this as vandalism. In technical terms, they are insufficiently versed in the relevant 'rule of recognition' (see 2.vi.c).

iii. Forgetting the rule

Distinguishable from failure to apply rules of recognition is the simple forgetting of rules, although in practice it is sometimes hard to tell the difference. Strong emotions or impulses can cause this forgetfulness. This is appreciated by courts in cases of violence which are explained by fear or provocation. Sexual excitement may also cause rules to be forgotten, although this is seldom accepted as a mitigation.

iv. Disapplying the rule

Even when the rule is remembered, and its relevance recognized, it is possible to decide that in the circumstances it does not apply. Dudley and Stephens, starving in their lifeboat, knew of the rule that they should not kill and eat a human being, but eventually decided to infringe it in order to remain alive.[3] Their decision was not that some other rule should be followed—a situation which is discussed later—but simply that in their situation it was irrational to obey the ban on murder. The rules of property, too, tend to be 'disapplied' in anarchic situations, of the kind which arise in the wake of military campaigns. Soldiers and civilians take food, fuel, and valuables which they know to be the belongings of others. The owners may have disappeared, or be regarded as enemies, or simply be in no position to assert their claims. This is sometimes called 'looting', but is distinguishable from the looting of shops and homes in a domestic riot, when the looters are aware that they are answerable to the law.

v. Exemptions from the rule

Rules of exemption have already been discussed in Chapter 2. They are not usually *reasons* for rule-breaking. A child under the age of criminal liability does not usually reflect, when stealing, that he is exempt, although a few juvenile thieves plead their age when caught. Diplomatic staff, however, frequently rely on their immunity when parking illegally or defrauding shops. In areas where it is known that the police seldom prosecute elderly shop-lifters this sometimes encourages them to take risks. More important, whole communities may feel that, although they are not exempt from the law of the land, they are under no moral duty to obey it, and see no benefit in doing so. Most countries have ethnic minorities which have seen themselves as persecuted, or at least denied equality. For them the laws of the majority lack the moral force which sociologists call 'legitimacy', especially when those laws run counter to those of the cultures from which the minorities came. Like diplomats, the minority demands the protection of the law without feeling that its members should obey all of its prohibitions.

vi. Private justification

'Necessity' is an example of what can be called 'public justifications' because they are, officially or unofficially, accepted as excusing or at least mitigating breaches of rules. Even more important are private justifications not recognized by lawyers but helping many a would-be law-breaker to reconcile what he wants to do with what he knows to be the law. He may acknowledge the legitimacy of a prohibition, and its moral force, yet be able to find a justification which sets his mind at rest. Shop-lifters can tell themselves that the shop can afford its losses, especially if they are under the impression that it is covered by insurance. People who neglect precautions against theft are said to be 'asking for it'. Rapists put the blame on their victims for provocative dress or behaviour. An all-purpose justification for common offences is that 'everybody does it in one way or another'.

Two sociologists, Sykes and Matza, drew attention to the importance of such 'neutralizations', as they called them, as long ago as 1957.[4] Unfortunately their article appeared in a very academic journal; and in any case scientistic explanations were then in vogue, so that 'neutralization' did not receive the attention it deserved. Private justifications have a subtle but wide-spread influence, even on criminologists and law-enforcers. As we shall see in 15.iii, some criminologists have emphasized the contribution of victims to the crimes from which they suffered; and at least one English judge has referred to the 'contributory negligence' of a raped hitch-hiker. Such justifications are not the inspirations of those who use them. Offenders learn them from parents, companions, or the mass media. Judges learn them from criminologists. The ultimate sources may even be the sayings of highly respected thinkers. Many a shop-lifting student can quote Proudhon's 'property is theft' (without reflecting that he himself is appropriating). Civil disobedience owes much to Dworkin's theory of individual rights.[5] Irish terrorists must be grateful to Bernard Shaw for arguing that 'nothing is ever done in this world until men are prepared to kill one another if it is not done'.[6] The Devil has all the best tunes. Thrasymachus talks more interestingly about law-breaking than Socrates. Machiavelli is better known than the virtuous Grotius. What they are remembered for are private justifications.

vii. Overriding rules

A rule may be regarded as overridden by another. Organizations such as the Mafia or the Hell's Angels are well known for rules which run counter to the criminal law. Less notorious are rules of loyalty to family, friends, companies, or political parties which persuade people to 'cover up' each other's misdoings. It is not only criminals who condemn tale-bearing. There are other sorts of overriding rules. Young men often feel obliged to react violently when they or their girls are publicly insulted. The violence need not be drastic, but must be immediate and visible to onlookers. The conventions of the vendetta are time-honoured, and followed not only by Sicilian peasants but also by football teams, colleges, politicians, book reviewers, and media personalities. Usually such justifications are permissive; but sometimes they are obligatory: retaliation and *omerta* are not only allowable but the only correct behaviour.

viii. Rule-breaking as a gesture

Rule-breaking is sometimes a symbolic action, intended to convey a message in a dramatic way. The message may be a denial of the rule-makers' right to regulate the actor's conduct, as for instance when children openly disobey their parents or teachers, or when demonstrators defy the instructions of the police. It may be a condemnation of the particular rule which is being broken, as when motor-cyclists *en masse* defied the law requiring them to wear safety-helmets. A third kind of symbolic infringement is what social workers sometimes call 'the cry for help': a more or less deliberate infringement by men, women, or children who seem to be trying to draw attention to their intolerable situations. The infringements—often consisting of minor shop-lifting or criminal damage—involve rules which seem irrelevant to their problems: their aim is to bring these problems to official or public notice.

ix. Rule-breaking for pleasure

Rule-breaking can be enjoyable. The enjoyment may lie in awareness of the risk of detection and its consequences. This is sometimes what motivates vandalism. It can be pleasurable, too, to watch the reactions of police, firemen and the public to a fire-alarm or a bomb-warning. Prestige can be earned on the spot by violence or defiance of authority. A subtler, more pathological excitement can be got from making sure that arrest is not merely risked but made certain: some female shop-lifters seem to seek detection, and are said to enjoy the manhandling and attention they receive. Some law-breakers, as Freud observed,[7] appear to be assuaging a vague sense of guilt by more or less deliberately incurring punishment.

x. Selective rule-following

What cannot be said too often is that rules, unlike natural laws, do not have to be obeyed. In a situation in which alternative rules justify different lines of conduct people are able to take their choice, in theory always, in practice often. However strong their allegiance to a rule, they can nearly always be induced to break it, especially if three conditions are fulfilled: a personal reason, a good chance of escaping detection, and a ready-made justification, usually in the form of some other rule. The more sophisticated the individual, the wider the range of justifying rules which he will have learned from discussions, reading, and attention to the media of information and fiction. And the more often he feels that he is disadvantaged by the rules of the criminal—or civil—law, the more attention he is likely to pay to justifications for disobedience.

Paradoxically, it is the human tendency to think in terms of rules and justifications which makes it so difficult to 'talk someone out of' repeated law-breaking. This is especially so when he belongs to a social group with whom he shares his non-conforming rules and justifications. Removing him from these associates usually involves associating him with another group; and if this is an incarcerated group it is unlikely that their rules and justifications will be any better. Concerned parents can sometimes 'rescue' a child from association with delinquent groups by transferring him from one school to another, or even by the drastic expedient of moving home; but this is usually out of the question. They may be able to discredit the rules of his delinquent associates, if they can discuss them dispassionately with him. An older brother or sister may be more effective in this way. But for many families the generation gap makes this very difficult.

xi. *The rationality of rule-breaking*

However great the variety of rule-breaking states of mind, most of them can be regarded as rational, given the situation of the offender or his special wants. He may borrow an unlocked car because he has missed the last bus to his home. He may have the knack of stealing goods which he cannot afford. He may need cash and know how to snatch a handbag, play a confidence trick, or sell stolen property. He may be a motorist in a hurry who realizes how little he risks by disobeying a traffic-light. He may be an employee, council member, doctor, or dentist in public service who sees how unlikely it is that false claims for expenses or services will come to light. He may be a leader or a would-be leader who hopes that judicious violence will ensure his ascendancy, whether through fear or prestige.

These kinds of conduct are irrational only if very strict criteria of rationality are adopted: for example, if rationality is defined so as to exclude risk-taking. Since that would also exclude a lot of legitimate commerce, not to mention highly enjoyable recreations, it is obviously far-fetched. What is not so far-fetched is the distinction between 'short-term' and 'long-term rationality'. Short-term rationality takes into account only the gains and losses which can occur in the immediate future: the other kind has a longer perspective. Yet this distinction too is questionable, not merely because the boundary between the short and the long term is obviously a vague one, but also because of its assumptions about the offender's future. If he has a secure job, a comfortable retirement, a settled family life to look forward to, long-term rationality has a meaning. If he has none of these, it may not mean very much, in which case short-term rationality is the only kind left.

xii. Risk-taking

What is arguable is that not all but some sorts of risk-taking make rule-breaking irrational. If what is risked is a very grave consequence—death, disablement, financial ruin—and the reward of the action is a short-lived pleasure or a minor economic gain, risk-taking may be called irrational. Even then, if the probability of the consequence is low, we hesitate to apply the label. Sometimes the probability is genuinely negligible. More often the actor has persuaded himself that it is. He may do so by taking precautions. Rock-climbers belay themselves to natural or artificial projections. These may in fact be firm enough to safeguard them if they fall; but sometimes they are what are called 'psychological belays', of doubtful strength. Persistent offenders too use psychological belays, and pin their hopes on clever lawyers, hesitant witnesses, credulous juries, and the doctrine of 'reasonable doubt'. Some people enjoy risk-taking more, not less, if the risk is substantial. Risk does not provide a clean-cut criterion of rationality.

xiii. Rationality and self-reproach

There is perhaps one criterion, however, which makes sense whatever the actor's circumstances: if his action is one for which he knows he will reproach himself morally soon after committing it. By this criterion some impulsive and many compulsive actions could sensibly be categorized as irrational. They can of course be carried out in complete forgetfulness of the actor's moral rules, but even so could be labelled 'irrational' if the criterion were that the actor in his normal state of mind would realize that he would feel guilty about them later. Whichever of these criteria is adopted, a definition of irrationality on these lines would still exclude most law-breaking, which is committed by people who do not feel guilty about what they have done, or at least not guilty enough to outweigh their motives for doing it. On the whole this favours the definition. 'Irrationality' is not a very helpful concept, and the more widely it is used the less illuminating it is.

xiv. Monolithic explanations

Since it is possible to distinguish at least nine states of mind in which rules are infringed, we should be very sceptical of 'monolithic' explanations of law-breaking. It is logically conceivable that all these states of mind are the effect of a single cause; but it is hardly probable.

Yet the medieval notion of a single origin of all misbehaviour dies hard. Idleness was declared by a statute of Henry VIII to be 'mother and root of all vices'. Modern single-factor theories are only a little more sophisticated. For Edward Glover, the psychoanalyst, the 'key to all problems of delinquency' was the unconscious need for punishment. Sociologists too can be worshippers of monoliths. For Sutherland, it was 'differential association'—the learning of criminal values from others—that was all-important; for Matza it was 'drift'; for Wolfgang subcultural values; for Lemert 'labelling'; for Fyvel 'insecurity'. Wilkins's 'general theory of deviance' depends on the notion of the 'amplification of deviant values' through social rejection by conformists.[8] The museums of criminology are full of such monoliths, covered with the runes of the faithful and the graffiti of the critical. Not all of these authors explicitly claimed that their explanatory theories were all-embracing. If challenged they might have conceded that some crimes did not fit. Wilkins, however, makes no bones about his theory: it is 'a general theory of deviance', and any multi-causal approach is 'an anti-theory' (which is apparently a bad thing to be).

Psychologists are less hopeful of achieving 'unifying' theories: their discipline demands experimental tests. Even Eysenck no longer claims that the difference between extraverts and introverts is of universal relevance. Yet psychology has occasionally erected minor monoliths to explain huge subdivisions of social behaviour. Dollard and Miller believed that the occurrence of aggressive behaviour always presupposes the existence of frustration and, contrariwise, that the existence of frustration always leads to some form of aggression.[9] In order to maintain this they had to talk their way round some awkward facts: for example that aggression is obviously sometimes the result of being attacked. Their answer was to call attack a form of frustration. This illustrates the reverence of psychologists for natural laws, and one way of dealing with phenomena which do not seem to obey them.

xv. Durkheim's rule

Admittedly the examples of monolithic explanation which I have given are no longer in vogue. Most are now recognized as the product of a process which might be called 'selective magnification'. Like art experts who apply lenses to an interesting part of a painting, sociologists and psychologists who achieve genuine insights into certain kinds of criminogenic situations occasionally magnify them to the exclusion of the rest of the canvas. Even those who resist this temptation, however, continue the search for natural laws of misbehaviour. When Dollard and Miller formulated their explanation of all aggression, or Cressey formulated his explanation of all embezzlement,[10] they were following one of Durkheim's 'rules of sociological method': 'to each effect there corresponds always a single cause'.[11] On this principle, one has only to define with sufficient narrowness what one wants to explain in order to be able to offer a single explanation which will fit all instances.

Durkheim's rule seems to work in medicine. If a disease is defined precisely enough it is possible to find a toxin, bacillus, virus, or endocrine imbalance which is found to be present in all cases. It would be more accurate, however, to say that when a disease seems to be sometimes attributable to X and sometimes to Y it is usually subdivided into two diseases, each defined by what is believed to be the main causative factor. As a taxonomic expedient—an educative way of describing diseases—this has its value. But when the expedient is applied to human actions its value is negligible. Durkheim applied it to human suicide by subdividing this according to its motivation. 'Altruistic suicides', for example, were distinguished by their altruistic states of mind. If one quibbles, and points out that there are several sorts of altruism—a willingness to die for one's country, or to die in order to save one's family from destitution or from disgrace—this is presumably met by further subdivision. It then becomes clear that what Durkheim's rule says is simply that one way of classifying human actions is by the actor's intentions. What he was not saying was that any sort of human action for which we have a name—such as 'suicide', or even 'altruistic suicide'—must have a single explanation. If anything he was warning sociologists against this fallacy.

Criminologists, too, need to think hard about the ways in which they define what they try to explain. Even those who realize that 'law-breaking' is too heterogeneous to be the subject of a single theory are still capable of treating 'violence', 'acquisitive dishonesty', or other wide subdivisions as if they were sensible *explicanda*. Yet as soon as it is plain how many different states of mind may lead to law-breaking actions it becomes obvious that at the very least such categories must be subdivided according to these states of mind. This is recognized when we talk about 'political homicides', 'jealous murders', or 'murder in the course or furtherance of theft'; and if as much attention had been given to shop-lifting as to homicide it would have been similarly subdivided.

xvi. Occasions

When formulating possibility explanations we cannot disregard what is usually called 'opportunity', but should more precisely be called 'occasion'. Law-breaking cannot occur without a situation which makes it *possible*. One cannot shop-lift where there are no shops. To call this 'opportunity' suggests a law-breaker who is on the look-out for a suitable target. Some people are certainly on the look-out for opportunities, and some are even 'opportunity-makers', who can set up situations which suit what they want to do. Yet many crimes are simply the result of a coincidence between an occasion and a state of mind. Hence the correlation between the number of cars on the road and the number of car-thefts, or the incidence of traffic accidents.

The explanation of a particular infringement must begin with an occasion which is perceived by the infringer as an opportunity. (His perception may of course be mistaken, in which case all that happens is an 'attempt'.) If the opportunity is real but not obvious, part of the explanation must account for his expertise in noticing it, or his persistence in looking for it. If he seems to be an 'opportunity-maker', this too must be explained. Yet criminologists have neglected the distinction between 'opportunity-noticers', 'opportunity-seekers', and 'opportunity-makers'. If the risk is more than negligible his readiness to take it must figure in the explanation. By this time we are involved in describing and accounting for his state of mind, which calls for a narrative covering some of the relevant preceding events. The narrative may be short, confined to a few minutes before a blow was struck or property stolen, or it may be a long 'case history'. To be satisfactory, however, it must explain not only why he saw the occasion as one in which he could (or should) act as he did, but why his state of mind was one in which he felt his action to be permissible (or obligatory).

This is the point at which the usual theories may be invoked. They are not always necessary. He may simply have forgotten the rule in a situation which makes his forgetfulness understandable. He may have been quite understandably ignorant of it. The situation may have been so extreme that almost anyone would have 'disapplied' it. The risk may have seemed negligible, given his appreciation of the situation or his experience.

Common sense, however, is not always enough, so that theories step in. They may trace his attitude to the rule back to his early upbringing, in which his parents' inculcation of respect for rules was faulty. They may point to the 'values' of the friends he made outside his family, or to the influence of television and other media of communication. Justifications of rule-breaking, and the symbolic uses of it, are almost always learned from others, whether peers, pop-stars, or political thinkers; and the media are obviously essential where pop-stars and politicians are the source. Very few law-breakers think of original justifications on their own. They may not have read Proudhon, Nietzsche, de Sade, de Quincey, Marx, Sartre, Shaw, Dworkin, or Leary, but they have picked up thoughts which are traceable to them.

That is not, of course, the whole story. 'Justified' and symbolic law-breaking are more likely in societies which are sharply split by politics, religion, ethnic groupings, or relative deprivation. At this point, however, we are no longer listening to an explanation of particular offences. Instead of being told why Jones did what he did, we are being told why property crimes (or symbolic violence, to take another example) are more frequent in this society than in that: an answer to a very different question. It is this sort of question which sociologists of crime are usually addressing. Their answers do not contradict narratives of the kind which explain particular law-breaking actions, although some sociologists write as if they did. Sociologists' answers even complement psychological case histories, for example when they explain why punitive or lax child-rearing methods prevail in this or that society, or why political justifications for homicide are popular in one society and unpopular in another.

The literature of criminological explanation is a vast territory, some of it over-cultivated, but some of it only vaguely mapped, or covered with sand-dunes of verbiage. To find one's way through it calls for the ability to see when different questions are being posed, and when irrelevant answers are being offered.

7

Sentencing and Not Sentencing

Efforts to reduce the frequency of offences, and the harm done by them, take many forms. People try to protect themselves and their property: a subject dealt with in Chapter 16. Identified offenders are disposed of in ways designed to discourage them or potential imitators: the subject of the next few chapters. Both sentencing and prevention are to some extent 'focused' measures, which concentrate either on the offenders or on their targets. From time to time, however, hopes have been raised by claims for less sharply focused measures, aimed at whole sectors of the population which were believed to supply most of the offenders. Free education, slum clearance, and the provision of recreational facilities for the young were inspired by humanity as well as self-interest; but among the hoped-for effects was the reduction of crime. A great deal was achieved; but not a fall in crime-rates. Religious leaders, moralists, and child psychologists made a more direct approach by trying to raise moral standards or to alter modes of child-rearing; and they received a considerable amount of assistance from the news media—in particular from magazines aimed at young mothers. What impact they had on the families which seemed most in need of their advice has never been estimated. Current campaigns take the more specific form of propaganda about the harm done by certain forms of law-breaking, such as drug-abuse and child-abuse. Their effectiveness may prove easier to measure.

i. Semi-focused measures

It would be unfair to dismiss these unfocused policies as completely irrelevant. Even if their effects have not been marked enough to be detectable in national statistics, they must have had some beneficial influence on the people at whom they were aimed. The fact remains that both official policy and public faith continue to place their trust in focused measures, directed at individuals. There was a period in the USA when a semi-focused approach made a bid for popularity. It seemed practicable to identify 'high-risk' categories of juveniles before they fell foul of the law, and to subject them to non-coercive forms of attention which would save them from this presumptive fate. Sheldon and Eleanor Glueck showed that by combining a few criteria it was possible to construct a 'prediction scale' which would distinguish fairly successfully between high-risk and low-risk children.[1] Their work was discredited partly by the ethical objections which were aroused by even mild intervention in the lives of high-risk families, partly by exaggerated claims for the accuracy of their predictive formulae, but partly too by the failure of the best-known attempt to put prediction into practice. This was the Cambridge-Somerville Youth Study, in which 650 matched pairs of 'likely' and 'unlikely' juvenile delinquents were either assigned to one of ten 'counsellors' or provided with no help of this or any kind. Counselling lasted for two and a half to eight years: some pairs were discarded to lighten counsellors' case-loads. The three-year follow-up was a disappointment: there was no evidence that counselling had reduced the juveniles' chances of getting into trouble.[2] In fact this was not a good test of the value of predictive selection, because the counsellors had no professional training for such work, and varied their approaches unsystematically; but it was regarded as the refutation of the Gluecks' approach. Nowadays efforts are concentrated on individuals who have been officially identified as having already broken the law. For the most part they are applied by criminal courts; but not always. An increasingly popular group of measures is known, generically, as 'diversion'.[3]

ii. Diversion

The offender may be offered an alternative to prosecution. The Inland Revenue deal with most detected tax-evaders by allowing them to pay what they owe plus a 'mitigated penalty'. Bad drivers, if lucky, may get away with a warning letter or a 'fixed penalty' fine. Drunks may be dumped at detoxification centres. Soliciting prostitutes get two cautions before being arrested (but kerb-crawling men do not). Drug addicts—not pedlars—may be offered treatment. Mentally disordered or senile offenders may be allowed to enter hospital, or become out-patients if their offences are trivial. Juveniles—especially girls, but also boys with clean records—may be 'cautioned', with or without supervision to follow. Diversion may be conditional—for example on attendance at a clinic—or unconditional, as it is when adults are cautioned in England. If conditional, it is revocable, and the offender may be prosecuted if he breaches the condition: if unconditional it is irrevocable, in practice if not in law.

iii. Prosecution

Even if prosecuted the offender may still be lucky. The evidence may not be enough for a finding of guilt, or only enough to convict him of a less serious offence than the one which he in fact committed. 'Under-conviction' may be the result of 'undercharging' by the prosecution, which may have decided to save itself trouble, or have entered into 'plea bargaining' with the defence. This is how reckless driving may lead only to a conviction for driving without due care and attention; attempted rape may become 'indecent assault'; murder may be reduced to manslaughter—a less culpable category of homicide. Whatever the charge, an offender who can put up a plausible defence has a good chance—under the adversarial system[4]—of an acquittal, partly because of the credulity of inexperienced jurors, partly because of the doctrine that 'reasonable doubt'[5] precludes a finding of guilt.

The defence may be mistaken identification: a single witness can often, under cross-examination, be got to admit enough uncertainty to give rise to reasonable doubt. It may be justification: for example that the taker believed he owned or had a right to what was taken. It may be lack of the essential intention; that he did not mean to deprive the owner permanently of his property, only to borrow it.[6] In cases of violence 'self-defence' is often the excuse, and 'defence of others' is also acceptable if the circumstances seemed to leave no reasonable alternative. Occasionally it is 'necessity'. The American Model Penal Code defines this as a situation in which 'the harm or evil sought to be avoided . . . is greater than that sought to be prevented by the law'.

English case-law, however, is much less generous, and much less clear. Another infrequent defence is 'duress', when the offender claims to have acted under a threat of death or serious personal violence. Provocation, so often the excuse in cases of violence, is not strictly speaking a defence, since it cannot lead to an acquittal, only to mitigation, or in cases of homicide to a conviction for manslaughter instead of murder. The same is true of 'diminished responsibility' due to 'abnormality of mind', which by statute in England (and common law in Scotland) reduces murder to a less culpable degree of homicide (in the case of other crimes sentencers can mitigate sentence in the light of psychiatric evidence). 'Automatism', on the other hand, is a complete defence: the plea that the apparent 'action' was a reflex movement, or that the actor was in an epileptic fit, or asleep, or in a semi-comatose state as a result of, say, hypoglycaemia. 'Insanity' is a defence of sorts, since it exonerates the offender while ensuring that he is committed to a mental hospital; but to amount to 'insanity' his mental disorder must satisfy strict criteria—so strict that in England this defence is very rare.

iv. The death penalty

Assume, however, that the offender has been found guilty of an offence. What can be done to him by order of a criminal court?[7] Some states still use the death penalty, usually for homicide, but sometimes for other offences, such as armed robbery (Nigeria is an example), serious economic offences (the USSR is an example), or drug-smuggling on a large scale (in Singapore, for instance). Even in Britain, where capital punishment for homicide was abolished in the 1960s, it is still in theory the penalty for treason and certain forms of piracy, although these charges are never used in peacetime. The effectiveness of the death penalty in preventing the offender from committing further crimes has never been questioned: its unpopularity is based on objections which are chiefly moral. In its strongest form the moral argument is that to execute someone deliberately is no more justifiable—and sometimes less—than the crime itself.[8] Retentionists usually reply that it is justifiable because it is deserved as punishment, at least when the crime is deliberate homicide without an acceptable excuse. Theological retentionists say it is good for the soul. The more pragmatic argue either that capital punishment is the only or the best way of preventing recidivism, or—in the case of terrorists—the taking of hostages by their colleagues, or of discouraging other people who are contemplating murder. Pragmatic abolitionists argue that it is no more effective as a general deterrent than long incarceration (evidence supports this) or that it transforms assassins into martyrs, alienates ethnic minorities who suspect discrimination, and is bad for the morale of prisons.

v. Other corporal penalties

Lesser corporal penalties are flogging (abandoned in most western countries, but not in Africa), amputation of hands (still practised in some Islamic countries), and reduced diet (still used as a punishment in some prison systems). Attempts are made from time to time to revive the popularity of flogging, or its juvenile equivalents; but the great majority of penologists regard it as more likely to brutalize offenders than improve them.[9] Castration and pharmacological inhibitors should be regarded as attempts at incapacitation rather than 'treatment', and are mentioned in Chapter 10 on that subject.

vi. Psychiatric and psychological treatment

Some drugs, however, are used not as inhibitors but in order to deal with mental disorders which seem to be responsible for rule-breaking. Depressive offenders frequently respond well to anti-depressive drugs, and also to ECT—electro-convulsive therapy. Lithium seems to improve not only sufferers from mania but also people who are apt to behave with impulsive violence. 'Conditioning' is also used, more often under the title of 'behaviour therapy', to help offenders to learn less antisocial ways of conducting themselves. Its demonstrable successes, however, seem to be confined to those whose rule-breaking takes a single, stereotyped form, such as fetichistic thefts; and even so relapses are reported after a time. Psychoanalysis and its descendants seem to be effective only when the rule-breaker himself has a strong incentive to co-operate, and is in any case both slow and costly in specialists' resources. The techniques of psychiatrists and psychologists vary from person to person. They may abandon one approach for another in the light of experience, or try different methods on the same offender. Consequently, courts are not empowered to order a specific form of treatment when sentencing: only to make an order which in effect hands the offender over to the experts. Even then, he is usually safeguarded by the law against 'hazardous or irreversible' procedures, unless he gives properly informed consent. The obvious example is psychosurgery, which—in Britain at least—is considered only as a last resort, and carried out only after patients, relatives, and independent experts have agreed that it is the only hope.

vii. Occasionalism

If the illness is regarded as more serious than the offence, the philosophy of most sentencers and psychiatrists is 'occasionalism'. The offender's conviction is treated as the occasion on which it is justifiable to allow the criminal justice system to hand him over to the health service. (Sometimes the criminal justice system retains control over his release; but more often this is left to the doctors.) Probation, too, is sometimes used in an occasionalist way (see 7.xi).

viii. Custodial sentences

But it is time to turn to more usual sentences. In many countries the most severe sentence that can be imposed is custodial.[10] The 'nominal length' of the sentence is specified by the sentencer, within the limits permitted by statute. In some countries the statutes set only upper limits, in others both upper and lower ('minimum-maximum' statutes); and in some they specify the proper length, allowing additions or deductions only for aggravating or mitigating circumstances. In England, and jurisdictions which copy England, the normal length of the nominal sentence is dictated by a 'tariff' or 'guide-lines' arrived at either by agreement between sentencers or by decisions of appellate courts. In the USA some jurisdictions follow the English model; but several have adopted the more rigid Continental type of statute.

All jurisdictions, however, allow or prescribe an indeterminate form of sentence for offenders who have committed very grave offences. Many prescribe 'life' for murder (as in England) or for murders which seem not to deserve the death penalty, as in some North American states. Most jurisdictions permit 'life' sentences (or indeterminate ones under some other name) if the sentencer regards the crime as sufficiently grave or the offender as sufficiently dangerous, but confine such sentences to certain types of offence. In a few jurisdictions 'life' means more or less what it says: that the prisoner is most unlikely to be released until at the point of death. More often the executive uses its power to release him, usually under supervision and specified conditions of conduct, with the threat of recall if he does not conform. In some jurisdictions the sentencer can specify the minimum period for which he must be detained before release becomes a possibility. In England the judge can recommend a minimum in cases of murder but not other crimes;[11] and Home Secretaries have declared that whether or not the judge has made such a recommendation they will not normally consider release before twenty years if the murders were of certain kinds.

The quality of life in custodial institutions varies from the tolerable to the brutish. Even affluent societies have gaols which are sordid, overcrowded, and unhygienic, and which fail to protect inmates against abuse by the worst of their colleagues. The very name of 'prison', 'gaol', or 'penitentiary' now conjures up a picture so evil that in the USA the term 'correctional facility' is preferred. It is true that a prisoner serving a substantial sentence will probably find himself in a pleasanter building, hardly if at all overcrowded, where he can work, take classes, play games, and socialize without fear of being beaten up or raped (so long as he does not provoke others). If he is not a likely escaper he may end up in an 'open prison', in pleasant country, where his freedom of movement is controlled by rules rather than walls, or even in a prison hostel from which he goes to work in the community. These are the places which prison administrators like to show to sightseers. But what the experienced penologist wants to see are the establishments where the majority of prisoners, who serve short sentences, are kept. They are crowded in threes, fours, or larger numbers into cells built for half that number, with primitive sanitation and little or no open-air exercise, spending only short periods—if any—at work, at classes, or in contact with non-offenders. The sheer volume of the turnover means that those responsible for their control, health, work, education, and welfare can devote very little time to the needs of individuals. The English system takes care to protect them against each other, chiefly by segregating those who are likely to be persecuted; but in some systems even short-term inmates live in fear of each other, and are dominated by the violent or corrupt. What are seldom shown to visitors, unless they are able to insist, are the cells where troublesome prisoners are put, provided only with the bare necessities for living, and deprived of anything that helps to pass the time. Necessary as segregation is when dealing with the most antisocial members of a law-breaking population, these are the parts of prisons which most require rethinking and reorganization.

Custody is not always used with punishment or public protection as its aim. The accused may be remanded in custody to ensure that he does not disappear, reoffend, or interfere with witnesses before his trial.[12] Fortunately or unfortunately, as the case may be, his trial may end in an acquittal, in which event a person whom the law declares innocent has already suffered incarceration. Some countries offer compensation when this happens; but they are countries in which acquittal is less frequent than in Britain. Most countries do not. A few set limits to time in custody before trial; some—like Britain—allow it to be deducted from the nominal length of a custodial sentence (if one is imposed). Most try to ameliorate the conditions of custody for untried or unsentenced prisoners. Yet in England 'remand wings' and 'remand centres' (the latter for young adults) are scarcely more tolerable than the accommodation for men serving short sentences.

Custody is used with other aims. One is coercion: incarcerating a person to induce him to do something. This is not the same as deterring him from doing something: a subject discussed in Chapter 9. Prison is used coercively when fine defaulters are committed to it: many pay up at that stage. Contemnors of court are also imprisoned, in order to induce them to apologize, or comply with a court's directions. A sentencer may decide on a custodial sentence in order to ensure that an offender receives treatment for a behavioural disorder, although few prison systems are effective at providing this.

Whatever the intended effects of incarceration, it is criticized for its unintended effects, on health, on personality, on family, and on one's prospects after release. There are undoubtedly prison systems in which food and hygiene are so inadequate as to damage physical health, although this does not seem to be true of most European systems. All systems expose some types of prisoner to the risk of violence from others: but so do offenders' ways of life outside. Nearly all prison sentences deprive a family of one of its members, and sometimes of its main earner, thus inflicting undeserved deprivations on spouses and children. The enforced separation is not always a tragedy: a short—or even a long—rest from the offender is sometimes good for the family. Social workers' efforts to prevent the break-up of families are not always in the interests of the wife and children; but with or without such efforts remarkably few marriages are destroyed by the prison sentence itself, unless it is a very long one, or the latest in a series.

A known ex-prisoner has more difficulty in job-finding than a man who has simply been fined or put on probation. Rightly or wrongly it is assumed that he is less likely to be a hard or trustworthy worker. Agencies which specialize in finding employment for such men have to concede that many are not good at holding down their jobs. Prisons, too, are said to be 'schools for crime'; and there is evidence that amongst men with similar records of offending those with more 'time inside' are more likely to be reconvicted. A man who has committed only one offence is unlikely to be turned into a criminal; but the others form friendships with recidivists and learn new techniques of dishonesty. It may well, however, be those very friendships and techniques which increase their chances of being identified and thus reconvicted. The friends they make are known to the police; and the techniques they acquire are those which are practised by unsuccessful criminals. If so, imprisonment merely makes them easier to reconvict.

What needs to be viewed with even more objectivity is the claim that incarceration damages mental health or personality.

Ordinary detention does not produce a schizoid, manic, psycho-pathic, or inadequate personality. Sometimes it provides the first opportunity for a skilled diagnosis of this sort, especially in cases of violence. More often the inmate proves to have a record of earlier diagnosis by clinics or hospitals. Not infrequently he is plunged into a depression by being locked up; but this is usually a realistic reaction to his situation.[13] Aggressive psychopaths may react even more explosively to the discipline of prison, or to the behaviour of their fellow-prisoners. A schizoid inmate may become even more withdrawn or paranoid; but this happens in mental hospitals too. The most that can be said about the mentally retarded is that they suffer more in prisons than they would in specialized institutions, and are less likely to get the care or treatment which they need.

Another claim, however, is that inmates who are not dis-ordered or retarded may become 'institutionalized': uninterested in the events of the outside world, and so accustomed to a regu-lated existence that they cannot take the ordinary initiatives of everyday life. This is more likely to be true of the minority who spend long periods in custody. Sapsford certainly found signs of this in some of his sample of English lifers. What has not been attempted is a clinical study of prisoners after release from long sentences—or indeed sentences of any length—to see whether such effects persist or disappear. Coker, who studied more than 200 ex-lifers in a non-clinical way, found no evidence of deterio-ration. After a short, sometimes restless, period of resettlement, they got and kept jobs—sometimes better than their former ones—made new homes, married or remarried. They showed 'a fierce desire for independence and a capacity to manage their own lives'. If they had become institutionalized during their years inside, it must have been a temporary adaptation.[14]

It is nevertheless an increasing awareness of the avoidable evils of prison life which has stimulated the anti-prison movement. Its extremists question the need for custodial sentences: its mode-rates want incarceration restricted to offenders who are really dangerous (a label which is discussed in Chapter 10). Even those who see imprisonment as an essential deterrent for offenders who are not necessarily dangerous, simply unresponsive to any other sentence, concede that far more money and professionalism should be devoted to prisons, and that the way in which they are run should be subject to searching investigations by 'inspectors' or 'ombudsmen' (as they already are in the better systems).

ix. *Release*

In most countries a prisoner serving a determinate sentence can qualify for release after serving a fraction of his sentence (in England two-thirds). This 'remission' is treated as the right of any prisoner who has not forfeited it by being found guilty of a disciplinary offence (or in some prison systems by failing to work hard). Release on remission is unconditional, and he is not—in Britain at least—subject to recall. Before his remission date, however, he may in many systems become eligible for conditional release. This is not treated as his right, but is administered selectively, and prisoners regarded as 'good risks' are the most likely to benefit. A prisoner paroled in this way is subject to requirements, including supervision by a probation officer (or 'parole officer' in the USA), and can be recalled for breaches, until he ceases to be 'on licence'. Normally this happens at the date when he would have been due for remission; but a lifer is subject to supervision for a very long period, and even after supervision ends is liable to recall until he dies.

Criticisms of prisons make no exception where release procedures are concerned. Not much fault is found with systems of automatic remission. So long as it is withheld only for specified breaches of rules, it is recognized that this is a useful incentive to good behaviour. If loss of remission is irrevocable it can fail to serve this purpose: a man who has lost all hope of getting out before the end of his nominal sentence has little else to fear, apart from segregation. The remedy, adopted in England and some other countries, is 'suspended' loss of remission, which can be restored after a period of good behaviour. Overcrowding has been seen as an argument for increasing remission, for example from one-third to one-half in Britain: but this has so far been resisted by politicians.

What has been subject to more attacks is selective release. Parole has been called 'resentencing'. The assumption seems to be that a period of detention specified by a court at the time of trial should not be subject to modification months or years afterwards. This assumption is easiest if one takes the retributive view that the original sentence is what is 'deserved'; but it also implies that the sentencer knows best what is deserved, and that his assessment would not, or should not, be affected by any later insight into the offender's personality, or by any change in his behaviour or circumstances. There are, however, other theories of punishment, and they are discussed in Chapter 8. A criticism of a similar kind is that if resentencing is allowed, it should not be done by people who are not sentencers. Some systems meet this by entrusting it to a judge (in France a *juge d'application des peines*); others by including judges amongst the groups of experts who decide when release can be allowed.

A criticism which begs fewer questions is that the criteria which govern such decisions are suspect. At best they consist of assessments of the nature and likelihood of further offending: a subject discussed in Chapter 10. At worst they are political, as when a minister refuses conditional release to a murderer whose crime has received a great deal of publicity in the news media, or when a parole board favours a prisoner because of the intercession of friends, as boards in the USA have been accused of doing. Decision-makers can counter such attacks by making public their criteria and their rules of procedure; but it is hard to convince prisoners or their sympathizers that these are always observed. Only an old-fashioned system which operated more or less automatically, with no scope for the consideration of special cases, would do that.

x. Financial penalties

The vast majority of offenders are not regarded as cases for custodial or specialist treatment, although some of them could benefit from it if resources allowed. They are simply fined, either by courts or by administrative authorities (an example being 'fixed penalties' for minor traffic offences). Fines have received remarkably little attention from penologists, who have tended to concentrate on sentences which are spectacular—capital, corporal, or custodial—or innovative, such as community service or reparation. It is only in the last few years that it has occurred to them to study a measure which is used far oftener than any other.

Fines have a number of negative virtues. They are less expensive than any other measure, and can even contribute to the high cost of law-enforcement if they are sufficiently large. They do little harm, except when an exorbitant fine imposes real hardship on a whole family, or drives the offender to raise funds by illegal means. Unlike such measures as suspended or deferred sentences (see 7.xii and 7.xiv), they do not give the impression that offenders are 'let off', although it must be conceded that small fines, such as 'fixed penalties' for illegal parking, seem to operate as taxes rather than deterrents where moderately affluent offenders are concerned. The difficulty of measuring their efficacy as deterrents will be discussed later (see Chapter 9); but when they are deterrents they have fewer unwanted side-effects than any other deterrent.

Most fines are of standard amounts, fixed with regard to a 'price-list' rather than the offenders' means or culpability. A few countries operate the 'day-fine' system, under which fines for serious offences are calculated as fractions of the offender's earnings; but even so for most offences the tariff still operates, and is not raised often enough to keep pace with inflation. Most English[15] courts take no steps to find out the financial standing of a defendant until he defaults in payment. Until that stage all they usually know is whether he is employed (or on a pension) and if so what his earnings (or pension) are. They are allowed to reduce their standard fine (which often varies from one magistrates' bench to another) if they are persuaded by the defence that it would be too harsh, but not to increase it when the defendant is obviously well off. One result is under-fining. Another is frequent defaults, so that they have to hold special 'means inquiries'.

In many cases the result of means inquiries is a reduction of the fine (an admission that it was excessive) or an extension of the time or number of instalments allowed for payment. If the offender seems to be simply unco-operative, or incompetent at budgeting, there are several expedients for extracting payment. Goods can be seized and sold; but this is more practicable when the offender is a small business rather than an individual.

Earnings can be 'attached', so that a fraction of them is paid to the court each week or month; but employers find this a nuisance. The offender can be searched on the spot; but if he knows this he can take care to empty his wallet before he presents himself. The High Court can be asked to allow the magistrates' court access to the offender's bank account; but this cumbersome procedure is used only when large amounts are owed. If no other expedient works, or seems likely to, the finee is threatened with imprisonment:[16] a stage at which he often finds he can pay after all.

At the end of the day, a small percentage of finees find themselves being taken to prison. The percentages vary from 10 per cent in the case of burglars and robbers to less than 1 per cent in the case of traffic offenders. Their periods of detention are short, and they can 'buy themselves out' at any stage by paying the appropriate fraction of what they owe: many do. Quite a number of fine-defaulters are simply experienced petty offenders who know just when to find the money, or who prefer imprisonment to payment. Some are so feckless, incompetent, or despairing that no method of collection would work, and the uselessness of imprisoning them is one of the features of the system which is open to criticism. Defenders of the system point out that the threat of custody is by far the most effective means of collection when offenders are able to pay, and would be weakened if exceptions were seen to be frequent. Another criticism is that unpaid fines result in imprisonment for 'non-imprisonable' offenders, such as drunks or soliciting prostitutes, and it is even said that courts use strict fine-enforcement as a way of imprisoning persistent offenders of this kind.[17] If the amount of the fine is deliberately fixed so that the offender is unlikely to be able to pay it, even by instalments, this is certainly contrary to the principle of the system. But there is no principle which forbids the imprisonment of non-imprisonable offenders who disobey a court order with which they are capable of complying. Other forms of disobedience can be punished with imprisonment, under the heading of 'contempt of court'.

xi. Supervisory measures

Offenders are fined on the simple assumption that this deters.

Much less simple are the assumptions underlying probation and community service. In Victorian England probation was a 'second chance' for a petty offender, and especially those whose offences were attributed to 'intemperance'. Instead of sentencing him the magistrates were persuaded to place him under the supervision of a 'police court missionary' or a private person of respectable status, to let him prove ('probate') that he could 'go straight'. In the early days only 'first offenders' of a petty sort were allowed probation, but as the police court missionaries developed into a professional service available to every court the measure was applied more generously. The first probation officers were for the most part religious in outlook, and many still are; but religion gave ground to psychoanalytic assumptions, which placed more emphasis on rapport between probationer and probation officer. The influence of Freud on American social workers had spread, via British psychiatric social workers, to social workers in general. Most English probation officers now see themselves as social workers of a specialized kind; and in Scotland the supervision of probationers is now one of the duties of social work departments. In England the 'generic' training for probation officers as well as social workers is the basic qualifying course, although some specialist instruction in criminology and criminal law is included. Psychology is now supplemented— indeed overshadowed—by sociology, of a kind that emphasizes the economic, educational, and environmental disadvantages from which many offenders suffer.

Nevertheless, probation officers see their role in different lights. For some the main task is to prevent the offender from reoffending, at least while he is under supervision. Judged by this criterion probation seems less successful with first offenders than fining; but probation officers argue that they are given the offenders who have 'problems'. This may well be so, since probation is rarely chosen by a court unless recommended by a probation officer's social inquiry report. Other officers would argue that preventing reoffending is not a fair criterion, since their main aim is to deal with the offender's problems: to improve his relations with his family, find him a job (or a more useful way of spending his spare time), cope with his drinking or gambling, and get him the welfare payments to which he is entitled. If so, probation becomes another occasionalist intervention, in which the conviction merely provides the opportunity for ameliorating the individual's condition.

Probation by itself is not always considered enough. In some Continental countries it is traditionally coupled with a suspended sentence, which may be financial or custodial. In England 'pure' probation has been the traditional form, carrying only the requirements to be of good behaviour, to tell the probation officer of changes of address or job, and to comply with his instructions for keeping in touch. In practice this has meant that probationers have short talks with their officers at intervals which vary from a few days to a few weeks during the currency of the probation order, which is usually two years but may be as short as six months or as long as three years. In recent years, however, probation orders have increasingly been coupled with special requirements, such as attendance for large parts of each weekday at 'day centres' where activities and even instruction in useful subjects may be provided.

xii. Community service

Another non-custodial measure is 'community service': the performance of unpaid tasks which benefit some section of the community,[18] for instance assisting staff or inmates in institutions, tending disabled people's gardens, clearing up after vandals, helping in youth clubs, nature conservation work. In England arranging and supervising community service is another function of probation officers and their ancillary staff: but in some other countries this is done by other social services.

xiii. Social inquiry reports

Supervision[19] and the administration of community service are not the only functions of probation departments. They also supervise parolees, and offenders conditionally released from hospital orders (see 10.vii). They undertake matrimonial conciliation in cases referred by courts. More important, they provide courts with 'social inquiry reports' (SIRs) on many of the offenders who appear for sentence. Information about criminal and employment records is supplied by the police, but for assessments of the offender, his family, and his social situation courts rely on the probation service. In countries without a service of this kind—such as Spain—it is left to defence lawyers (if any) to perform this function. Not even in England is every offender the subject of a report. It is hardly ever called for in the case of a traffic offender, a tax-evader, or anyone else who is almost certain to be fined, whereas if a custodial sentence is a real possibility a report is expected, and sometimes persuades the court to choose a non-custodial measure instead. What effects SIRs have on the efficacy of the system is not yet clear;[20] but when they are used they force the court to see the offender as an individual rather than as an item on a conveyor belt.

xiv. Nominal measures

A group of non-custodial measures can be called 'nominal' because they do not impose any specific penalty or obligation on the offender. An absolute discharge—or its equivalent in other jurisdictions—virtually declares that though the offender is technically guilty his offence was so trivial or pardonable in the circumstances that anything more would be excessive. A 'conditional discharge', on the other hand, warns the offender that if reconvicted within a specified period he will be sentenced for the original offence, as well as for the subsequent one. 'Binding over to keep the peace (or be of good behaviour)' has a similar effect, with the important difference that it can be used to deal with acquitted offenders and even witnesses, if their conduct seems to have contributed to a disturbance. In Scotland an offender can be 'admonished': that is, censured but not otherwise punished, so that the effect is to combine absolute discharge with slight disgrace. Deferment of sentence, on the other hand, tells the offender that he will be brought back for sentence in a few months, and that the severity of the sentence will depend on reports of his conduct (and sometimes on his fulfilment of promises made by him in court). Also regarded as a nominal measure by many is the suspended sentence of two years' or less imprisonment, which does not take effect unless within two years the offender is reconvicted of an offence for which he could be imprisoned.[21] But if the sentence is only partially suspended he must serve part of it: the effect is rather like that of a guaranteed parole without post-release supervision.

xv. *Controlling sentencers*

In jurisdictions where the use of punitive measures such as incarceration, flogging, and fining are subject to a statutory tariff, and exceptions are limited to well-defined circumstances, the result is a high degree of consistency between different courts. Anglo-American systems, in which sentencers are allowed choices, both in the kind and the severity of the measure, apply them with much less consistency. The assumption that inconsistency is incompatible with justice has led to various expedients for controlling sentencers without resorting to statutory prescription. Systems of appeal to higher authority—at first the head of State, later appellate courts—have been extended so as to deal with sentences as well as convictions. Sometimes—as in Britain and the USA—they are one-sided, and allow only the defence to appeal against a sentence which is claimed to be excessively or unnecessarily severe. In most other jurisdictions the prosecution too is allowed to appeal, especially if the sentence seems inadequate. In either system the result is control by case-law. In some jurisdictions of the USA judges have adopted a system of self-regulation by 'sentencing guide-lines', which are based on statistics about their own practice. The English Magistrates' Association from time to time provides its members with tables which amount in effect to a tariff of penalties for common offences, although it always adds that these can be varied to suit circumstances. Not all benches of magistrates, however, feel bound by these; many regard local circumstances and local practice with more reverence. The result is parochial consistency, but considerable variations between parishes: a situation which is acceptable to their publics, but criticized by academic penologists. What consistency means will be made clearer in Chapter 11.iii and 12.x.

8

Sentences and Justifications

The suffering caused by capital, corporal, and custodial penalties makes people so uneasy that there is a whole literature about the justifications for penalizing offenders.[1] The deliberate infliction of unpleasant experiences seems to call for some sort of justifying argument. When surgeons and dentists cause pain we accept this because their aim is to do us good; but what is the justifying aim of penalties?

i. Instrumentalism

The answer given is sometimes instrumental, sometimes non-instrumental. When it is instrumental the aim offered is usually the reduction of the likelihood of further offences, either by the penalized offender or by people who may be minded to act like-wise. The likelihood is meant to be reduced by eliminating or incapacitating the offender, by doing things of which the memory will discourage him ('individual deterrence') or by using him as an example to discourage potential imitators ('general deterrence'). If he is young the hope may be that a custodial or supervisory regime will alter his disposition so that he will lose the desire to behave violently or dishonestly, or at least be able to control it ('reform').[2]

The trouble with these instrumental aims is that they are not always achieved. Elimination is undeniably effective. Incapacitation by custody is effective so long as it lasts. But the efficacy of deterrence and reform is much more debatable.

ii. Corrective efficacy

The responses of individual offenders to their sentences are not easy to assess. What they themselves say is not always reliable. They may claim to be reformed by probation, yet be rearrested within a month. They may tell an interviewer that they will never again risk going to prison, and yet return soon after release. Or they may deny being afraid of detention, yet take trouble to avoid reconviction. Nor are probation or prison staff much better at diagnosing the effects which they have on their charges. They are apt to talk about cases which stand out in their memories because of their unusual features; and they are likely to be swayed by faith or cynicism. Penologists prefer statistics, especially if the numbers are large enough to reduce chance effects to negligible proportions.

As usual, they cannot count exactly what they would like to: the 'successes' of sentences. There are several reasons for this. Even on the assumption that not reoffending is the criterion of success (an assumption that will be discussed shortly)

(*a*) it is by no means always certain that not reoffending is due to the sentence. It is sometimes due to the shock of arrest and exposure, sometimes to the efforts of relatives after the trial is over. It is safer to talk about the 'failure-rates' of sentences than their 'success-rates', although even this over-simplifies. Some offenders come from—and return to—environments so unpropitious that only blind optimism would expect the sentence to keep them out of trouble for long.

(*b*) it is seldom possible to be sure whether an offender has or has not reoffended, unless one is dealing with a very specific sort of offence, such as incest or wife-beating. By following up offenders in official records we can categorize them as reconvicted or not (or rearrested or not, as in the USA); but we can be sure that an unknown number of the 'not reconvicted' have merely committed offences without being identified. Those who are reconvicted tend to be the more repetitive or incompetent.

(*c*) there are also 'counting problems'. If a man is sentenced for burglary should he be counted as a failure if he is reconvicted—or cautioned—for reckless driving? Some would say 'Yes: he hasn't learned to respect the law'; but most would say 'No: all the sentence could be expected to do is to cure him of burglary.' Yet they would probably regard a later conviction for robbery or fraud as a sign that the sentence had not been a complete success. What penologists tend to do when studying reconvictions is to distinguish only broad groups: violent offences, sexual offences, dishonest acquisition, illegal ways of driving, drug-related offences.

(*d*) there are also follow-up problems. Tracing reconvictions is not always easy. Most centralized systems record only offences which fall into categories regarded as important (in England 'standard list offences'; in the USA 'felonies'). Minor traffic offences, offences of drunkenness, and breaches of regulations such as those dealing with payment of local taxes are noted only in local files. The period of follow-up also raises problems. If one is comparing a sample of custodially sentenced offenders with a sample of probationers, obviously the follow-up of the prisoners should begin only when they are 'at risk': that is, have been released. But should the probationers be followed up only for the period of probation—which may be as short as six months or as long as three years—or should it cover a period after they have ceased to be under supervision? Even a follow-up which deals satisfactorily with this problem has to end at some stage: but how long should the 'period at risk' be? British studies suggest that if a violent or dishonest offender is not reconvicted within five years it is unlikely that he will be after that. Sexual offenders, on the other hand, have a low five-year reconviction-rate, but their likelihood of reconviction does not decline so sharply: some are reconvicted ten or more years later. (The explanation may lie in the large number of sexual offences which are not reported by victims.) In spite of these facts, most researchers seem content with follow-ups of two years, and sometimes less. They—and the policy-makers interested in their findings—want quick results. 'Art is long, life short': but not short enough for penology.

iii. Reliable findings

Yet in spite of all these awkwardnesses reconviction statistics undeniably succeed in reflecting several differences so consistently that they cannot be dismissed as telling us nothing. If that were so, how could the following findings, repeated in many samples in many jurisdictions, be explained?

(*a*) males are more likely than females to be reconvicted. (So the sexes must be distinguished in such studies);

(*b*) the more offences an offender is known to have committed, the more likely he is to be reconvicted. 'Nothing predicts behaviour like behaviour', as Kvaraceus once said;

(*c*) those who are convicted of certain types of offence are more likely than others to be reconvicted, though not necessarily for the same type of offence. Burglars are more likely to be reconvicted than sexual offenders;

(*d*) after the peak age for the type of offence, which is usually in the middle or late teens, the likelihood of reconviction declines—slowly—with increasing age.

The trouble is that when penologists look for differences of such magnitudes amongst offenders subjected to different sorts of sentence, they do not find them. To be more precise, they find them, but when they make the necessary statistical allowances for sex, type of offence, previous convictions, and age, such differences as might be attributable to the nature of the sentence vanish or are greatly reduced. For example, in England those fined for standard list offences have lower six-year reconviction-rates than those put on probation; but if women and men in their teens are excluded, and allowance made for type of offence and previous convictions (which are commoner amongst probationers than finees) the difference is small.[3] Other studies also suggest that if allowance were made for employment it would be smaller still (unemployed men are less likely to be fined, but more likely to be reconvicted).

iv. What works?

The failure to find substantial and consistent differences between the reconviction-rates for sentences of quite distinct kinds—custodial, financial, supervisory—led Martinson to question whether they had any effect on offenders' law-breaking.[4] Martinson has been credited with popularizing what is called the 'nothing works' assumption. In fact even his original article conceded that there were 'isolated' examples in which some way of handling offenders had apparently made a difference to their recidivism, although it was usually impossible to identify exactly what feature had made the difference. In a later article (unfortunately published in a much more obscure journal) he more or less retracted the sweeping assertions of his 1974 article, and conceded that 'treatment will be found to be important under certain conditions, beneficial under others, and detrimental under still others', a statement with which it would be difficult to disagree.

'Nothing works' is an over-simplification of what even Martinson said at his most pessimistic. In the first place, an equally justifiable inference from the evidence would have been that 'nearly everything works'—but to more or less the same extent. This is not only prima facie more likely: it is more consistent with the findings of the better follow-up studies. It is very difficult to evaluate the effects of sentences on teenagers because so many of them are left in, or quickly returned to, the families, companions, and environments which made offending so natural. But so far as adult men in England are concerned the picture is slightly clearer:

(*a*) adults with a lot of previous convictions (that is, more than four) for standard list offences have such a high probability of being reconvicted (nearly 90 per cent) that it makes no difference whether their sentences are financial, supervisory, or custodial.

(*b*) adults with fewer or no previous convictions are more likely to be reconvicted if given a suspended prison sentence than if imprisoned, fined, or put on probation. This is quite inconsistent with the inference that 'nothing works'.

(*c*) the exception to (b) is men put on probation for their first conviction, who have high reconviction-rates. The explanation may be either that they are selected for this measure by courts, on the advice in probation officers' reports, because they seem to present special problems, *or* that probation seems so mild a consequence that they are encouraged to be optimistic about the consequences of reconviction.

v. *'Time inside'*

Research in California and Florida has been interpreted as showing that the length of time spent in custody makes little difference to rates of rearrest or reconviction.[5] Tables in the annual statistics of the English Prison Department seem to contradict this, since they show lower two-year reconviction-rates for the longer sentences.[6] Neither interpretation is conclusive. The Florida research drew a crude distinction between men released before serving eighteen months, and those detained longer. The Californian research distinguished burglars who had served more than, and less than, forty-five months. They left open the possibility that considerably longer sentences do have an effect on reoffending. On the other hand, the Prison Department's statistics which seem to support this fail to make allowances for age, type of offence, previous convictions (if any), or time spent under supervision after release (which may have been longer in the case of the longer sentences). Until more thorough research has been carried out it is not safe to say whether longer sentences have more effect on recidivism than shorter ones.

Nevertheless, pessimism about the effect of the choice of sentence on recidivism is at the moment so strong that those who justify sentences instrumentally tend to rely on two other instrumental effects: the incapacitation of the offenders and the deterrent and educative impact which sentences have on potential offenders. These are the subjects of the next two chapters.

9

Deterrence and Education

Whatever effects the sentencer expects to have on the future conduct of the offender, he must also have in mind the likely effects of the sentence upon the conduct of other people. The effects which sentencers most often hope for are deterrence and education.

i. General deterrence

Many legislators as well as sentencers believe that the penalties which courts impose discourage potential imitators. Research in the last two decades or so has shown that this sort of discouragement affects fewer people, or lasts for less time, than used to be assumed: but it has not justified the statement of some critics that 'deterrents never work'. This is prompted by dislike of deterrents rather than hard evidence. The dislike is understandable: the use of a deterrent means the deliberate infliction of hardship, if not harm; and if the benefit is invisible and unquantifiable— as it must be when unidentifiable people are deterred from offending—it is not easy to weigh it against the visible penalizing of an identified individual.

ii. A fallacy about the death penalty

This is especially so when the penalty is drastic. When the advocates of capital punishment offered deterrence as a justification for it, one result was to associate deterrence with inhumanity in people's minds, so that it was assumed that all deterrents involve the infliction of irremediable harm, which need not be so. The other result was that when the opponents of capital punishment pointed to statistics which showed that the availability or non-availability of the death penalty was not associated with differences in homicide rates,[1] a naïve inference was drawn: that the death penalty does not deter anyone. The most that could be inferred was that the death penalty deterred *no more* potential homicides than the substitute for the death penalty, which is very long imprisonment. Not only are most homicides committed in a state of mind in which the likely penalty is not a consideration; even when it is considered, it seems, the prospect of being incarcerated for a very long time discourages *as many* (if not always *the same*) people as the prospect of being executed. This may sound unlikely to people who feel sure that they would choose incarceration rather than execution; but there is no contradiction. It is fallacious to assume that in order to deter an equal number of people deterrents need to be equally feared. They need only be sufficiently feared. Pedestrians stop for motor cycles as well as buses.

iii. Demonstrating ineffectiveness

The argument that deterrents do not deter because the death penalty does not seem to affect homicide rates is thus based on a misinterpretation of statistics. Nor have other attempts to show that deterrents never work been much more successful. This would in the nature of things be a very difficult thing to demonstrate. To deter someone from doing something is to influence him by a threat or threats so that he refrains from doing it, postpones doing it, does it somewhere else, gets someone else to do it,[2] or finds some other way of achieving his desire. To demonstrate by statistics that the use of a deterrent is not having *any* of these results would obviously be very difficult.

iv. Demonstrating effectiveness

On the other hand, it is occasionally possible to point to demonstrations that some potential offenders are discouraged from some types of offence by the threat of legal consequences. Sometimes these demonstrations are accidental results of abrupt changes in the likelihood of detection. When police forces are put out of action—as they were for seven months in Nazi-occupied Denmark—there are spectacular increases in reports of robberies and thefts, but not of frauds and embezzlements; and on the rare occasions on which other police forces have been on strike similar increases have been reported.

Conversely, an abrupt increase in what seems to be the likelihood of detection has been shown to have a beneficial effect on the frequency of driving under the influence of alcohol. The introduction of breath testing[3] in Britain in 1967 was followed by a marked drop in serious road accidents, especially on weekend evenings, when most heavy drinking takes place. What was also demonstrated, however, was that the effect of a spectacular technological innovation of this sort may wear off with time. Drivers who liked to drink heavily probably came to realize that their likelihood of being detected and convicted had not increased quite as sharply as they had thought. Either drinking drivers became acceptant of a higher recognized risk, or experience reassured them that the risk was not as great as they had thought (or both processes took place). A similar wearing-off seems to take place when drivers are warned by signs that speed traps are in operation.

v. Subjective probabilities

Findings such as these emphasize that—at least where such traffic offences are concerned—the occurrence of deterrence depends on creating and maintaining an impression of a high risk—technically called a 'high subjective probability'—of detection and conviction. What happens when police forces are out of action suggests that the same is true of acquisitive offences when the chances of detection depend on rapid police action, as they do in cases of robbery and most thefts, but not true of frauds and embezzlements. Penologists have generalized such findings into the proposition that without a high subjective probability of detection deterrence will not occur. Some go so far as to add 'however severe the penalty', although the evidence for that is far from impressive.

Even the most limited assertion cannot be regarded as a universal truth. At least one experiment seems to have demonstrated the occurrence of deterrence when the subjective risk of detection was far from high and when no attempt was made to raise it. Schwartz and Orleans arranged interviews with nearly 400 Illinois taxpayers.[4] These were divided into four matched groups, whose interviews differed in content. The 'sanction' group were asked questions designed to remind them indirectly of the penalties which they might suffer if detected in tax-evasion. The 'conscience group' were asked instead questions designed to arouse their civic sense and feelings of duty. The 'placebo group' were asked only neutral questions which avoided both these topics. The fourth group were not interviewed at all, in order to see whether even a placebo interview produced some effect. The interviews took place in the month before the taxpayers were due to submit their statements of income for 1962. Without disclosing information about individuals the Internal Revenue Service compared the returns of the four groups for 1961 and 1962. The reported gross incomes of both the 'sanction' and the 'conscience' groups had increased in 1962, whereas those of the 'placebo' and uninterviewed groups had slightly decreased. In short, both the attempts to produce more honest tax returns, by appeals to conscience and by reminders of penalties, seemed to have succeeded.

This experiment is interesting because it is usually assumed that taxpayers have a low subjective probability of being detected in understatements of their incomes, and because no attempt was made to raise their subjective probabilities. It is of course possible that the mere mention of penalties in the questions put to the sanction group raised their estimates. Another possibility is that when an offence involves armchair decisions, with every opportunity to weigh the consequences of an event, even the consequences of a not-very-probable event have more influence than they do in the case of offences such as drunken driving or speeding. Finally, a more general point must be made about the proposition that deterrence does not occur without a high subjective probability. It would be more precise to say 'without a sufficiently high level of subjective probability', and admit that we have no basis for knowing what is a sufficiently high level. The threshold must vary from one individual to another, and be affected by his experience, his anxiousness, the situation, the degree of deliberation with which he decides to commit or refrain from the offence, and the strength of his desire to commit it.

vi. 'Undeterribility'

We need to be reminded not only

(*a*) that different kinds of offence are committed in very different states of mind, with or without planning, impulsively or compulsively, and from a wide variety of motives;

but also that

(*b*) some people are restrained from yielding to impulses, compulsions, or motives not by fear of law-enforcement but by what psychologists call 'internal restraints', meaning usually the thought of the guilt or shame which they would feel if they yielded;

and also that

(*c*) some people are 'undeterrible' so far as some kinds of offence are concerned, so that even a very high subjective probability of detection does not restrain them.

'Undeterribility' has hardly been considered as a subject of investigation, although it is exhibited by many chronically recidivist prisoners. It is not of course a single or simple state of mind. Some violent offenders are simply unable to control their tempers, especially when they have been drinking. Some offenders are in the grip of addictions, compulsions, or mental disorders which preoccupy them to an extent that excludes thoughts of penalties. Some have experienced imprisonment so often, and have so little acquaintance with pleasanter ways of life, that the prospect of another sentence is merely depressing rather than discouraging. Some seem to be over-confident, so that even experience does not convince them of their incompetence. Some have every justification for their confidence.

vii. *The nature of the penalty*

Important as the subjective probability of detection is, it cannot be inferred—as it sometimes is—that the nature of the consequences of detection is unimportant. There is evidence that the rates are lower where the probable sentences are longer.[5] Again, Norwegians and Swedes believe that their compliance with prohibitions on drinking and driving are largely due to the fact that detection usually means a short prison sentence.[6] What is doubtful is whether legislation which merely makes tougher sentences *permissible* has much effect, at least in England, where courts have their own norms. Even when tougher measures are made obligatory, as has happened with disqualification from driving, courts seem very ready to be persuaded to make exceptions.

viii. General versus individual deterrence

It is at this point, however, that the distinction between general and individual deterrence becomes important. General deterrence is any discouraging effect which threats have upon people who might otherwise commit offences; individual deterrence is the discouraging effect of actually experiencing what is threatened. A sentencer is often confronted with an offender who seems either undeterrible or unlikely to break the law again: yet he may feel obliged to consider the need for general deterrence. In practice this usually means that he imposes the 'tariff' penalty for fear that if he is more lenient the number of people who commit similar offences will increase. When he reasons thus he is assuming that the news of his sentence will reach a substantial number of potential but deterrible offenders. In fact, the chances that the case will be reported by the national news media are very small, unless it involves a spectacular crime or a well-known person. It has a somewhat better chance of being reported by local newspapers; yet even so it is not the sentence which makes an impression,[7] but the nature of the offence and the identification of the offender by those who know him.

ix. Publicized leniency

The important exception is a choice of sentence which strikes the news media as extremely lenient. When a woman is put on probation for the manslaughter of a husband or lover, or when a rapist is merely fined (see 15.iii), considerable publicity is likely. But whether cases of this kind weaken any general deterrent effect is doubtful. Public criticism of the sentence—whether ill-informed or not—may well have the effect of emphasizing that the usual penalty is a substantial prison sentence.

What the sentencer must seriously consider is whether he is sentencing an offender with criminal acquaintances who will take note of any leniency. Some offenders belong to social networks (see 4.xiv) along which the news of their sentences travels with much more speed and precision than through the perusal of the *Criminal Statistics*. If a sentencer takes this into account he has to face a moral question. Is he discriminating unfairly if, having evidence that the offender belongs to a criminal network, he rejects mitigating considerations which he would otherwise take into account? The moral issues raised by a policy of general deterrence are discussed later.

x. Exemplary severity

As for occasional severity, even more scepticism is justified. The 'exemplary sentence', designed to impress potential imitators with courts' determination to discourage this or that sort of crime, has been approved by the English Court of Appeal. Essentially, it consists of an exceptionally severe sentence imposed in the hope that people who are minded to commit similar offences will believe that the courts have adopted a more severe sentencing policy, even when that is not so. The evidence which supports this hope is anecdotal and weak. Often cited is the sentencing of nine young men to four years' imprisonment for their involvement in attacks on Asians and Blacks in the Notting Hill district of London in 1958. The sentences were exceptionally long, and were not only meant to be exemplary but were claimed to have put an end to racial violence in the area, at least for some time. This interpretation is far from reliable. The original attacks seem to have been prompted by an inflammatory racialist broadsheet, and may have died down because a document of that kind goes out of circulation and has only a temporary effect. There was also increased police vigilance. The nine youths sentenced may have been the ringleaders, whose removal would thus account for the diminution of violence. Finally, racial violence in the area did *not* cease completely after the sentences.

Nevertheless, the Notting Hill sentences are still cited, nearly a third of a century later, in support of exemplary sentencing. A sounder anecdote, combined this time with a genuine attempt at measurement, was provided in 1973, when a Birmingham youth was sentenced to twenty years' detention for a particularly brutal mugging. Because of its exceptional severity the sentence was well publicized in the local as well as the national Press. Yet when the week-by-week frequencies of muggings in Birmingham, Liverpool, and Manchester were studied by Baxter and Nuttall, no decrease could be found in the weeks following the sentence.[8] This does not *prove* that exemplary sentencing is ineffective. The most that can be said is that it is hard to find a properly documented instance of its effectiveness.

xi. *The state of knowledge*

It is not possible in a single chapter to review the enormous literature of research into the effectiveness of deterrents.[9] But some general comments can be made. Naïve beliefs both in the effectiveness and in the ineffectiveness of a policy of deterrence have been replaced by the less exciting realization that for *some* length of time *some* people can be deterred in *some* situations from *some* types of conduct by *some* estimation of likelihood that they will be penalized in *some* ways; but that we do not yet know enough to enable us to be very specific about the time, the people, the situations, the conduct, or the subjective likelihood or nature of the penalties. Equally important is the lack of knowledge about methods of manipulating people's impressions of the probability or severity of penal consequences. We can be fairly sure that they are not altered by statistics about clear-up rates or the use of fines or custodial sentences. Apparently they can be altered by publicity about technical improvements in methods of detection, such as breathalysers; but this effect seems to weaken with time. In any case, it would be useful if we could be more specific about the sort of people whose impressions both need to be and can be manipulated. They do not include people who refrain from the conduct in question for reasons other than the expected consequences of detection: for example, for moral reasons. Nor do they include the 'undeterribles' discussed in 9.vi. It is a third group, which has been called the 'marginally deterrible', whose inclination for the conduct can be affected by such considerations.

xii. *The role of the news media*

What is fairly clear is that the news media's choice of what to report about clear-up rates and sentences is not designed to further a policy of general deterrence; and that it is only occasionally possible to make deliberate use of newspapers, television, or radio for this purpose, usually by paying for the publicity.[10] This fact, coupled with the vagueness of our knowledge about the operation of deterrents, should dissuade both legislators and sentencers from being very optimistic about this function of penalties.

xiii. Moral aspects

Practical considerations apart, deterrence is sometimes attacked on moral grounds, although these too need a critical scrutiny. The moral case would be unanswerable if it were certain, or highly likely, that what are intended as deterrents do not in fact deter. They would then be nothing but the deliberate infliction of suffering or inconvenience for an end which cannot be achieved. We have seen, however, that the present state of knowledge does not support so categorical an assertion.

Consequently, moral objections must take a more sophisticated form.[11] It is possible to concede that deterrents are effective sometimes or quite often, but to argue that they involve sacrificing the interests of the person penalized to the interests of others.[12] It is not a complete answer to point out that the penalized offender himself sometimes benefits from being deterred. Too often the offender is undeterrible, and the only justification for the penalty is either the deterrence of others or the plea that he deserves the suffering. Those who accept desert as a justification for punishment (a possibility discussed in Chapter 11) are thus able to claim that they are not merely using the offender as a means of frightening others, but are according him the dignity of being treated as a responsible person.[13] For those, however, who do not regard just deserts as a good or sufficient reason for inflicting suffering, it is harder to be sure that the penalty is anything but the use of the offender as an exhibit *in terrorem*. If the penalty is meant to have beneficial effects on character—as some people claim for community service—or if it is accompanied by treatment of a disorder (as a hospital order is), consciences may be salved. But it is difficult to claim that sentences of imprisonment confer such benefits; and fines can only be deterrents or retributive punishments.

xiv. Two kinds of deterrent

The moral objectors to deterrents should also, however, make the important distinction between those which do and those which do not inflict serious and lasting harm. In the former category are capital punishment and physical mutilation. In the latter are fines, which inflict temporary inconvenience, or at most deprivation, but hardly ever lasting harm. There are much stronger moral objections to the infliction of lasting harm than to the imposition of a temporary deprivation, although discussions of the morality of deterrents seldom make the distinction. This escapes notice because it is usually imprisonment which is assumed to be the deterrent, and because it is assumed that it does serious and lasting harm (an assumption which has been questioned in 7.viii).

xv. Educative effects

Independent of beliefs about deterrent efficacy are theories about the educative function of sentences: that is, the possibility that a sentence of a certain kind can affect people's 'tolerance' or 'moral evaluation' of the offence for which the offender is sentenced.

These theories—which take different forms—must be distinguished from the claim that the mere prohibition of this or that kind of conduct, by means of the criminal law, influences moral attitudes. There is experimental evidence which strongly suggests that this is so, at least in the case of some types of conduct and some types of people (see 14.iii). For sentencers, however, who have to take the criminal law as it stands, the question is not whether moral attitudes are influenced by the fact that, say, failing to use a seat-belt is an offence: it is whether such attitudes are influenced by the sentence.[14] A subsidiary, but important, question is whether attitudes are altered by publicized sentences which are markedly more lenient or severe than the norm.

xvi. The Sargeant effect

The belief that the penalty performs a symbolic (or 'expressive') function of this kind has been popular for nearly two centuries, not only amongst English lawyers but also amongst sociologists of a Durkheimian outlook.[15] More recently it has been seriously discussed by philosophers of punishment.[16] For English sentencers, however, the version which is most important must be that of the Court of Appeal in Sargeant's case.

There is however another aspect of retribution[17] . . . it is that society, through the courts, must show its abhorrence of particular types of crime . . . The courts do not have to reflect public opinion. On the other hand the courts must not disregard it. Perhaps the main duty of the court is to *lead public opinion*. (my italics)

The clear implication is that sentences should—at least when likely to be publicized—be of such a kind as to 'lead public opinion'; that is, presumably, to increase public disapproval of the offence in question.

Mrs Marsh and I experimented in an effort to detect the 'Sargeant effect' on adults' disapproval of five kinds of offence: domestic violence, vandalizing a telephone kiosk, a public-house fight, setting a dangerous booby trap for a thief, and a computer fraud which netted £7,000 in very small amounts from bank customers.[18] To maximize realism respondents were shown faked newspaper cuttings which described the incidents. Some sub-samples were told that the offender had been given a prison sentence of six months; some that he had been put on probation; some that 'people like yourself' disapprove strongly of the offence; some that they disapproved a little; some that the judge took a serious view of the offence; some that he did not. They were then asked to show, on a seven-point scale, how much they themselves disapproved. The results did not provide any support for the belief that the disapproval levels of substantial numbers of adults were raised or lowered by information about the sentence, or about the judges' views. Respondents' disapproval levels were overwhelmingly determined by their own assessment of what they read.

It is arguable that one should not expect the Sargeant effect to manifest itself as a result of a single newspaper report; and that the experiment does not refute the belief that a series of reports of similar cases in which offenders were severely or leniently sentenced would have this effect. Perhaps it would: but the news media are more selective than this in their choice of stories for publication. Nor is it usually the nature of the sentence which makes news: more often it is the unusual circumstances of the offence or the identity of a well-known defendant. Consequently, the news media do not report a series of similar sentences for similar offences. If the Sargeant effect is a genuine possibility it is a possibility that is most unlikely to be realized, because of the attitude of the news media to sentences.[19]

xvii. 'Anti-impunity'

The Sargeant effect, however, is not the only possible educative function. Gross offers what he calls an 'anti-impunity' version of deterrence as a justification for penalizing offenders:

According to this theory, punishment for violating the rules of conduct laid down by the law is necessary if the law is to remain a sufficiently strong influence to keep the community on the whole law-abiding . . . Without punishment . . . the law becomes merely a guide and an exhortation to right conduct . . . Only saints and martyrs could be constantly law-abiding in a community that had no system of criminal liability . . . The threats of the criminal law are necessary, then, only as part of a system of liability ensuring that those who commit crimes do not get away with them. The threats are not laid down to deter those tempted to break the rules but rather to maintain the rules as a set of standards that compel allegiance in spite of violation.[20]

Although the claim would be hard to test, it seems very likely that penalties do perform this function: that is, that they maintain allegiance to the rules of the criminal law by demonstrating that they are not infringed with impunity. This is a comforting thought for sentencers who are disillusioned about the efficacy of deterrence. It implies that the important audience so far as sentencing is concerned consists not so much of the likely offenders as of the people whose marginal deterribility or moral restraint, as the case may be, needs reinforcement now and again.

What Gross also believes, however, is that it is this function which is the *only* sound justification for penalizing offenders. One important consequence of such symbolic theories should be emphasized here.[21] This is that the justifying function of penalties would be achieved by merely pronouncing sentence and leading the intended audience to believe that it was carried out. If so, the infliction of harm which is involved in a prison sentence or a fine would not be justified, except to the extent that it is needed to maintain the belief that sentences are in fact carried out. That would justify the actual carrying out of sentences in only a minority of cases, chiefly those which received—or could be given—publicity. We must therefore distinguish between symbolic theories which consist merely of a claim that sentences convey important messages to the public, and those which also claim that this is the only, or the main, moral justification for attaching penalties to law-breaking. It is possible to believe in the anti-impunity effect (though hardly in the Sargeant effect) while holding other views about what justifies sentencing.

10

Incapacitation and Dangerousness

Uncertainty about the achievement of other instrumental aims has driven penologists to interest themselves in the only one which seems easily achievable: the incapacitation of the offender. It can be guaranteed by putting the offender to death. It is more or less assured by sentencing him to long periods of incarceration. Escape-rates are not very high, and during incarceration the offender's scope for harm is more or less limited to his fellow-inmates and the staff of his institution.

i. Non-custodial precautions

There are less drastic—and less effective—expedients for incapacitating some kinds of offender. Reckless, drunken, or incompetent drivers can be disqualified. Originally the justfication for this was pure incapacitation. Nowadays courts use it and see it as a penalty. Even the English Court of Appeal has referred to it as a 'punishment'. One result has been that periods of disqualification have become quite short: nearly three-quarters of all driving disqualifications imposed by English courts are for a year *or less*. It is also impossible to be sure what percentage of disqualified drivers refrain from driving. The indications are that those who are otherwise law-abiding—the great majority—obey the court's order, but a substantial minority are detected in driving while disqualified, usually as a result of another traffic offence. The Chicago practice of paying occasional visits to the homes of disqualified drivers to find out whether they were driving was very exceptional, and makes great demands on manpower. Impounding the cars of disqualified drivers would obviously be slightly more effective, but would be open to the equally obvious objection that it would inflict vicarious punishment (see 11.vi) on dependants.

Other illegal activities can be prevented—again with less than complete success—by disqualification. Ex-prisoners are refused permission to have firearms. Delinquent medical practitioners and pharmacists can be 'struck off the list' by their professional bodies. Dishonest businessmen can be debarred from being 'company directors', although this does not prevent them from managing commercial undertakings with other people as figureheads. Teachers who molest pupils can be blacklisted by the Department of Education and Science. Corrupt politicians can be excluded from public offices. These are only examples.[1] All of them have some reductive effect, but most can be evaded by one expedient or another if the offender is willing to risk detection and a short prison sentence.

There are other methods of incapacitation. Some sexual offenders can be prevented from repeating their offences if they are surgically or chemically castrated. Surgical castration is permissible in some countries if the offender consents, as he sometimes does in order to secure release from a long prison sentence; but it is very rare nowadays, at least in civilized countries. Chemical castration is carried out by means of drugs which abolish or greatly reduce sexual desire, but has two disadvantages. One is its possible side-effects on the offender's health, which call for careful monitoring. The other is that the offender can discontinue the treatment by simply failing to present himself for further doses, so that unless he is subject to supervision and control he may allow his harmful impulses to reassert themselves. As an alternative to incarceration, therefore, chemical castration is not a guarantee of protection. The same is true of drugs which reduce impulses to violence, such as lithium.

Children who suffer from sadistic or neglectful parents can be protected by being removed to foster homes. A striking fact, however, is the reluctance of social workers to use this power, usually because of optimism about the possibility of transforming bad parents into good ones. Courts, too, have shown an exaggerated respect for parents' rights, although in modern theory it is the welfare of the child which is the overriding consideration. The result is that several children die each year in spite of the fact that their hazardous predicaments are known to social service departments. Many more, only a little more fortunate, survive an affectionless upbringing in which neglect, cruelty, or sexual abuse are frequent. Legislators have provided social workers and courts with the powers to protect them; but the notion that separation from one's natural parents is always traumatic dies hard. So do the children.

There are other expedients. Equipment needed for a specific type of crime—such as a poacher's net—can be confiscated, although it is usually easy to replace. In France offenders can be subjected to an *interdiction de séjour*, which forbids them to visit a specified locality—such as Marseilles—or type of establishment, such as casinos. Proposals to give English courts a similar power have proved unwelcome both to the police and the probation service, because it is said to be unenforceable. (The French police were not consulted.) Drivers who are addicted to alcohol can be persuaded—but hardly compelled—to take a drug which will make them sick if they yield to their craving. Foreign offenders can be deported, Scots can be sent back to Caledonia, Welshmen to the Principality, Californians to California: but this merely relocates the risk, and often only for a short time.

Supervisory measures—at least of ordinary kinds, such as probation—are not effective incapacitators. The reconviction-rates of offenders *while undergoing* probation are as high as those of offenders after release from custodial sentences.[2] Californian probationers, too, seem to have very high reconviction-rates.[3] It would be unrealistic to expect a probation officer who has been trained to 'advise, assist, and befriend', and who seldom sees his probationers more than once a week, for less than an hour, to be able to exercise much restraint on their activities. The addition of requirements such as 'curfews' (permissible in the case of juveniles), residence in hostels, daily attendance at special centres, or involvement in special activities must to some extent reduce opportunities for law-breaking; but most English probation officers are opposed in principle to strict enforcement of such requirements.

There have been experiments in which offenders have been kept under surveillance of one kind or another while at liberty. They are not literally watched, but their whereabouts are checked at intervals throughout each day, either by radio devices attached to them or by human monitors who get in touch with them by telephone or visits. Both kinds of monitor can of course be shaken off. In at least one English city[4] helpers have been used to 'track' delinquent teenagers in this way, but without marked success in keeping them out of trouble. Radio devices have obvious shortcomings, since determined offenders can remove them. Even if they are not removed, and the offender is noticed hanging around a forbidden locality, such as a children's playground, it takes time for a police car to be summoned to the spot.

ii. Incarceration

In short, given the present level of human resources and efficiency, and the present attitude of most civilized countries to the death penalty, the only effective incapacitator is custodial. Moreover, it can be effective only if the offender is detained until he is unlikely to repeat his offence: otherwise the outcome may be merely postponement. Not that the value of postponement is always negligible. Deferring a burglar's next burglary for a year or two will not make much difference to the burglary statistics or—more important—people's anxieties about burglary. But when the offender is given to personal violence or sexual molestation, putting him out of action for some years will often relieve a whole locality of anxieties. In some cases even relatively short periods of incarceration will afford real protection to particular individuals: examples are men who have a grudge against their wives, fathers who commit incest with daughters, and young men who harass Asian shopkeepers.

Ironically, the problems raised by protective sentencing are more acute in countries where sentences are on the whole short. Where long terms of actual custody are normal for serious offences, both dangerous and non-dangerous offenders are kept out of circulation for substantial periods, and are older and wiser when released. But when short terms are normal it becomes necessary to have special protective sentences for a minority of offenders, unless the 'anti-protectionist' stance is adopted without exception.

iii. Anti-protectionism

Anti-protectionism has to be taken into account both as a climate of opinion amongst liberals and as an arguable policy. Its arguments take two forms, practical and ethical. The practical argument is logistic. The numbers of people who repeatedly steal, defraud, rob, vandalize, drive dangerously, or sell harmful drugs are so numerous that most societies could hardly afford the resources needed to keep them in prison for very long terms, to say nothing of the social effects which that might have. The most that can be afforded is the selective custodial incapacitation of much smaller numbers of offenders, chosen because they are regarded as likely to cause serious personal harm if set free. In practice, however, not even experts are accurate in distinguishing those who would repeat their harmful behaviour from those who would not. Those who would not are more numerous than those who would; or at least so it is said, on dubious evidence. It is petty offenders who are predictably repetitive: drunks, indecent exposers, careless drivers, pilferers. Consequently, from the point of view of prevention, the majority of long protective sentences are unnecessary, and therefore mistakes. Fewer mistakes would be made if there were no protective sentences at all.

The ethical argument is even simpler. Since deserts set limits to the severity of the penalty for an offence (see 11.v), a term of imprisonment which exceeds that limit in order to prevent a possible repetition of it is unjustified. As a Swedish committee put it, the offender is being punished not only for the offence he has committed but also for one he has not committed and may never commit.

The superficiality of the ethical version is obvious. It begs two questions, by assuming first that there must always be retributive limits to the length of a prison sentence; and second that the only proper function of a prison sentence is retributive punishment. The first assumption would be granted by a large number of people, but it is not logical to take it for granted: it is not axiomatic. The second assumption needs to be supported by an argument which the anti-protectionists have not supplied. Even if it is granted that imprisonment is normally used with retributive intention, or subject to retributively fixed limits, they have not shown why should it not—also or instead—be used with other objectives in mind.

The logistic argument also conceals a gap in its reasoning when it points out that, so far as really harmful offenders are concerned, fewer mistakes would be made if there were no prolongations of custodial sentences for the purpose of protecting other people. In the first place, this is now a doubtful claim. Recent—and sounder—research in England and California has shown that it *is* possible to identify categories of men whose reconviction-rate for robberies and other forms of crime involving violence is substantially greater than 50 per cent, so that their prolonged detention would involve fewer mistakes than their release.[5] Secondly, an argument which relies on counting the number of mistakes assumes that all mistakes are equally deplorable. Yet the mistakes involved in deciding whether to release or retain are of two quite different kinds. One involves releasing a number of offenders who will again inflict serious harm on members of the public. The other involves retaining a number of offenders who if released would not do so, but who cannot be distinguished at the time of decision from those who would. Most people would consider that the first kind of mistake is much more serious. Counting the two as simply 'mistakes', and glossing over the difference, is a dishonest use of arithmetic.

Some—for example the Floud Committee[6]—would add that offenders who have inflicted serious harm on people have given society the right to use sentences for the protection of the public. The public has to bear the risk of being assaulted, raped, or otherwise wronged by people who have hitherto shown no disposition to commit such offences. It has no right to demand someone's incarceration because his mere existence contributes to this general risk. People must be allowed a 'presumption of harmlessness' unless and until they have forfeited this right. But they forfeit it when they show, by proved conduct, that they have failed to obey the rules against such conduct. Society then has the right to 'redistribute the risks', to use the Floud Committee's term. This does not imply a *duty* to impose a long protective sentence: a right is not a duty. What it does imply is that in such cases courts have a duty to *consider* whether to exercise the right.

The anti-protectionists have an answer of sorts to the Floud Committee's argument, again a logistic one. The vast majority of homicides, rapes, and other serious assaults are committed by people with no previous convictions for such crimes: that is the 'general risk' which the public has to accept. The number of such crimes committed by people who have already been imprisoned for similar crimes is small in comparison. Most of them are released after serving the period of custody considered appropriate for their crimes. If all, instead of most, were released at that stage, and not detained for protective purposes, the increase in the general risk to the public, it is argued, would be negligible.

A lot depends, however, on what percentage is called 'negligible', and how it is estimated. American researchers—but none in England—have tried various means of estimation. One of the difficulties is that while it is easy to identify crimes that could have been prevented by longer detention when those crimes have been officially traced to people with previous convictions, it is not so easy in the case of unsolved crimes. No doubt some of these were committed by people previously sentenced for other crimes, and some by people who were not; but in what proportions? The best study at the moment is probably Greenwood and Abrahamse's (1982), which used not only the officially recorded crimes but also the self-reported crimes of penitentiary inmates in California.[7] Using self-reports and other information about the careers of incarcerated robbers (and other sorts of offender) they calculated that a 15 per cent reduction in California's robberies could be achieved by identifying 'high-rate robbers' and lengthening their sentences. It cannot be assumed that equal gains could be achieved in every jurisdiction. In Texas, for example, where sentences were longer, and robbery-rates lower, the researchers found that the gains would be less striking. The important point is that no calculations of this sort have even been attempted in Britain.

iv. What sorts of harm?

This still leaves a number of issues open. An important question is 'What kinds and degrees of harm justify protective sentencing?' In some jurisdictions—especially in the USA—the answer is 'any sort of felony, provided that there is evidence of a tendency to repeat it'. Other states list only certain felonies, such as murder, attempted murder, robbery, rape with force or violence, arson, kidnapping, sexual offences against children, and train-wrecking. English law permits 'life' sentences for some forty kinds of offence, ranging from trading with pirates to attempted murder. In some jurisdictions long protective sentences are not merely allowed but mandatory for certain crimes, such as murder or the sexual molestation of children. Usually the law allows sentencers to be selective in their use of protective sentences. In England the life sentence has, in the last fifteen years or so, been used only for ten kinds of offence,[8] and even then only when the offender seemed—to the judge at least—to represent a danger. On the other hand, when there has been evidence that the offender was mentally ill, mentally impaired, or psychopathic, special psychiatric orders for indefinite compulsory detention have been used for a somewhat wider selection of offences, some of which do not carry 'life'.

This anomaly raises another question. Should protective detention be used only when the offence which has been committed is itself very harmful, or should it be used when a not-so-harmful offence brings to notice a person with obvious indications of a greater-than-average probability of committing a really harmful offence, of the kind which is accepted as justifying protective detention? Must we wait until the really harmful offence is actually committed? In cases of mental disorder courts are less hesitant to act protectively; and British civil law allows psychiatrists to arrange compulsory detention in order to safeguard other people against the patient, without a court's authority and without the commission of an offence. By contrast, if there is no evidence of mental disorder courts hesitate to sentence protectively. Part of the reason is that the other sort of expert whose evidence is acceptable is the probation officer, who is often against custodial measures on principle. Police evidence at the sentencing stage is usually confined to the defendant's previous convictions, cautions and employment record. Mere statements that he is likely to do more serious harm are rejected unless supported by legally acceptable evidence. The result is that men—and sometimes women—who are regarded as dangerous by everyone who knows them receive suspended sentences, probation orders, or fines for acts of violence which were minor only because of the good luck, the skill, or the intelligent precautions of the victim.

v. *Indeterminate detention*

Another issue concerns the indeterminacy of most sentences of protective detention. The British 'life' sentence allows the executive to release the offender after any period, from a few months to many years.[9] The 'double-track sentence', devised by the Edwardians and copied by several European countries, obliges the offender to serve a fixed term for his offence, followed by a period intended for public protection, the second period being usually fixed, with the possibility of release before its end if this seems justifiable. Common in US jurisdictions is the 'semi-determinate sentence', with minimum and maximum terms set by statute or by the court within statutory limits. Even ordinary determinate sentences, however, can be used protectively when the judge is prepared to name a longer term than usual for the offence itself, a practice which the English Court of Appeal has approved in recent years. Ordinary fixed sentences, on the other hand, are eligible for remission and parole, so that they are, in effect, only semi-determinate.

Indeterminacy is logical when protection is a consideration. It is hardly ever possible at the time of trial to name a date by which the offender will have ceased to be a danger.[10] The objections are that great uncertainty is inflicted on the detainee, and that release may be delayed excessively by an executive which is over-cautious or influenced too much by public concern. Determinacy, on the other hand, sometimes means the obligatory release of someone who is still dangerous. In theory this can to some extent be remedied by strict powers of supervision and recall to custody; but it is usually—if illogically—regarded as improper to extend such powers beyond the term of the sentence, and in any case, as we have seen, supervision is a weak safeguard.

vi. *'Is he still a danger?'*

The central difficulty when release is being considered is finding any means of telling whether the offender has become less likely to repeat his sort of crime than he was when sentenced. Behaviour in custody is not usually a reliable indicator. There are no opportunities for child-molesting in prison, and even when female staff are accessible they are usually under male surveillance. Men who are violent towards other men are not only under surveillance but also mindful of the consequences of attacking a member of staff or a fellow-prisoner. (The official consequence is usually delayed release, but the unofficial consequence may be violent retaliation.) Occasionally it is possible to observe improvement. A man who behaves violently in the early part of his sentence may gradually learn how to control himself. A sexual offender may respond to treatment, or agree to submit to hormone implantation after release. The circumstances which led to his crime may disappear, as happens when the daughters of an incestuous father have left home.

Anti-protectionists emphasize the extent to which dangerousness depends on circumstances. Few men are dangerous as soon as they emerge from the prison gates. They need time to start heavy drinking again, to find criminal associates, or to form a new relationship with a sexual partner. It is often said that a man whose only act of violence has been the killing of his wife is no longer dangerous because he has no wife. But wife-murderers not infrequently marry again, or cohabit, and sometimes the relationship again develops into violence. Some offenders gravitate unselfconsciously into the kinds of situation in which they committed their earlier crimes. And some are conscious 'opportunity-makers' (see 6.xvi): for example child-molesters who apply for jobs in charge of children. Anti-protectionists, however, argue that the only way to avoid mistaken releases altogether is to detain such offenders for the rest of their lives: an answer which they regard as a *reductio ad absurdum*.

vii. Procedural problems

Procedural problems, too, beset release-decisions. Should they be taken by a judicial authority—as in some European systems—or by the executive, usually on the advice of a non-judicial board of experts and laymen, as in England and some US jurisdictions? If by a judicial authority, should the decision be justifiable on legal principles, for example as regards the onus of proof and the acceptability of evidence? Should the onus lie on those who represent the defendant's interests, or on those who think it unsafe to release him? If the decision, or the advice, rests with a parole board or some other non-judicial body, should the prisoner have the right to appear or be represented before it, or to be told everything that is said or written to it, so as to be able to challenge prejudicial statements? The English system is an odd, almost inconsistent, combination. The Mental Health Review Tribunals which decide whether to release patients from mental hospitals are quasi-judicial, allowing the patient to appear and be represented, but not bound by ordinary rules of evidence and with no clear principle as regards the onus of proof. The Parole Board which considers the release of both lifers and prisoners serving semi-determinate sentences is non-judicial in its proceedings, although it includes judges amongst its members. Prisoners do not appear before it, and are not represented. Unlike Mental Health Review Tribunals it does not take the decision to release: only to give advice in favour of release, which the Home Secretary can, and sometimes does, reject. On the other hand, if it decides to advise against releasing him, even the Home Secretary is not free to do so. The parole system is a safety-catch, devised by legislators who feared that the Home Office would take risks. In practice, the political consequences of unfortunate releases are so serious as to make administrators and ministers more cautious than tribunals.

viii. Regimes

Some criminal justice systems are more selective than others in their use of protective sentences, and readier to release offenders from them. Where all systems fall considerably short of justice is in the conditions of detention. If a person is being detained longer than is justified by the crime itself, and if the extension is for the benefit of others, it seems to follow that during the extension the regime should not be in any way punitive, but should on the contrary be as tolerable as is consistent with the denial of freedom. I know of no prison systems which genuinely honour this principle. The best of them allow long-term prisoners more amenities than short-term inmates; but that is not saying much. Even the liberal and much-praised Swedish prison system treats its high-security prisoners *less* humanely than the rest.

11

Desert and Ritual

The usual alternative to the instrumental aims discussed in the last three chapters is the retributive justification. This has a long tradition behind it, but in Anglo-American penology was eclipsed for nearly a century by Benthamite utilitarianism. Its renewed popularity in recent years is directly attributable to the undermining of faith in the corrective and deterrent efficacy of sentences. The new name of the old god is 'Just Deserts'. The old god is revered by at least three major religions—Judaism, Christianity, and Islam—and has inspired some terrible doings in his name. This may be why his American neophytes have found him a new one. Yet neither a grim history nor a new name is a sound reason for apostasy or conversion. The case for retribution as the main justifying aim of punishment has to be considered on its merits.

i. The essentials of retribution

Essentially, retribution consists of the deliberate infliction of death, suffering, hardship, or at least inconvenience, not because of any hoped-for benefit such as the reduction of misbehaviour but simply because the misbehaviour 'deserves' it. What 'deserving' means will be discussed in due course. If the penalty is to qualify as retribution in the strict sense

(*a*) it must be inflicted on the person who is believed to have misbehaved. It is true that Jehovah is said to have 'punished' the children of sinners, and that some devotees of Islam regard themselves as inflicting just punishment when they kill or maim the families or even the fellow-countrymen of people who have sinned against them. But this is called 'vicarious punishment', which is disapproved by Christianity and modern Judaism, and is regarded as a *pis aller* even by those who do not reject it.[1]

(*b*) it must be inflicted deliberately. Harm, suffering, hardship, or inconvenience which is simply the natural consequence of the misbehaviour does not qualify. A reckless driver who injures himself is not punished thereby. It is true that some European jurists call this *poena naturalis* ('natural punishment'), in order to argue that he is 'punished enough' by the natural consequences; but the very fact that they make the distinction implies that genuine punishment is a deliberate infliction.

(*c*) it must be inflicted by the decision of a human being (or a supernatural being) who regards what he is inflicting as deserved punishment. A dog which bites someone who is treating it cruelly is not really punishing. Nor is a sentencer who has instrumental aims in mind. Herbert Hart[2] adds that the decider must be someone other than the offender; but it is not easy to see why a conscience-stricken offender who inflicts suffering, hardship, or inconvenience on himself by way of atonement is not to be regarded as punishing himself in the most literal sense.

(*d*) it must be inflicted for a specific breach of a rule. Inflicting harm on someone simply because he is regarded as wicked, deviant, or unpleasant is something else. Hart and some other philosophers add that the rule must be a 'legal' one; but they are thinking jurisprudentially. It seems wrong to exclude, for example, penalties visited on children by parents for breaches of family rules. Most parents do this with instrumental aims, but some do it for retributive reasons.

(*e*) it must, say Hart and his colleagues, be 'imposed and administered by an authority constituted by a legal system against which the offence is committed'. This was meant to exclude 'unofficial punishment'—for example by vigilantes. But again it excludes the penalizing of children by retributively minded parents, unless perhaps Hart and his colleagues regard parents as having legal authority to do this. Suppose, too, that a group of people not constituted by a legal system have rules and penalize members who infringe them, not for instrumental reasons but because they 'deserve it'. Perhaps Hart would say that the operation of a system of rules makes this 'a legal system' in miniature. It would be at least clearer, and probably closer to retributive thinking in practice, to say that to qualify as punishment penalties must be imposed by persons given the right to do so *by some system of rules*. This would not exclude all 'vigilante justice', since vigilantes may have rules; and this may be regarded as an objection by those who—understandably—see vigilantes as a danger. The desire, however, to discourage practices should not distort definitions. It is quite consistent both to call vigilantes' penalties 'retributive punishment' and to argue that *they* should be discouraged from imposing them.

ii. Limiting retributivism

What definitions of retributive punishment do not tell us is why the infliction of it is justified when, by definition, it need not serve any instrumental aim. Some retributivists compromise at this point, and make it clear that so far as they are concerned the infliction of suffering, hardship, or inconvenience *must* be instrumentally justifiable; and that retribution merely sets upper (and perhaps lower) limits to what can be done to a person in the name of correction, general deterrence, or incapacitation. He should be punished 'to the limit' only when this seems justified by a likely reduction in misbehaviour. 'Limiting retributivism' raises two questions:

(*a*) how does it arrive at and justify its limits? Since this is essentially the same as the problem of uncompromising retributivism it will be discussed under that heading;

(*b*) does it meet the needs of those who have resorted to retributivism because they accept the view that instrumental aims are not achievable? A limiting retributivist who said that it did would in effect be arguing that penalties should never be imposed.

iii. Prescriptive retributivism

The uncompromising form of retributivism—the 'just deserts' point of view—asserts that penalties should be imposed whether or not they are instrumentally desirable, and even if they are undesirable. They should be imposed because they are deserved. There are both primitive and sophisticated versions. In the former what 'deserves' is the harm done: in the latter what 'deserves' is the harm intended, so that attempts deserve even if unsuccessful, while unforeseeable accidents do not. Secondly, while equal culpability deserves equal punishment, sophisticated versions recognize that the same punishment may inflict different degrees of suffering, hardship, or inconvenience on offenders of different ages, health, or economic status, so that consistency does not necessarily entail exactly similar penalties.

Even a sophisticated version of prescriptive retributivism, however, has difficulty in explaining what is meant by 'deserving'. It can say that when the penalty is deserved this means that it is imposed because of the offence; but this does not tell us why the offence is a reason for imposing it. When they try to explain this most retributivists resort to metaphors. For example

(*a*) the penalty is said to 'annul' the offence; that is, to bring about a state of affairs in which it is as if the offence had not been committed. Note that they have to say 'as if', because nobody can be unkilled, unraped, or unburgled. It is sometimes literally possible to undo the *harm* done by the offence, usually by the restitution of stolen property or the repair of damage, whether by the offender or by some other agency (compensation does not of course have the effect of undoing the harm). But penalties inflicted on the offender do not normally undo what he has done, and are not intended to.

(*b*) the offender is said to 'pay his debt to society' by suffering a penalty. In no literal sense, however, is there a debt to pay; only a fiction that society (or the family, or whatever) is owed something for the breach of its rules. Literal debts are never literally paid by the debtor's suffering.

To label an explanation as metaphorical is not of course to discredit it conclusively. A religious retributivist could argue that he was trying to express a God-given feeling that there was something right about retribution, but that he could not put it into literal terms. This might be acceptable if there turned out to be no literal explanation which made sense: but several have been offered, and at least one makes sense.

Kant, for example, is said to have believed that by penalizing the guilty supernatural displeasure is averted.[3] Whether Kant thought this or not, it is an incomplete explanation because it does not tell us *why* a supernatural being's displeasure at the commission of an offence would be averted by penalizing the offender. At most it merely implies that the supernatural being thinks retributively, but does not tell us any more than it would tell us about a human retributivist's reasoning.

There have been better attempts. For example, it is suggested[4] that offenders should be penalized because by breaking the rules they have gained an unfair advantage over the law-abiding, and fairness requires that they be disadvantaged. This is not so much a metaphor as an unexpressed analogy, the analogy being a game in which an unfairly taken advantage leads to the imposition of a disadvantage, such as a free kick. It is in the nature of an analogy that it does not correspond at all points to what is being explained; and that is what turns out to be the case with this one. Suppose that someone tries to commit an offence without succeeding, or having succeeded derives no advantage from it. Do we, like a referee, say 'no advantage, play on'? We do not: if we are sophisticated retributivists, we think that he deserves a penalty.

iv. *Retribution and rules*

There is one genuinely literal explanation, however, which makes very good sense.[5] It not only provides a rational reason why offences should be penalized: it accounts for retributivists' feeling that they should, and is thus a psychological as well as a logical explanation. As Chapter 2 made plain, man is a rule-making, rule-following animal. If the set of rules which has been breached includes a prescriptive penalizing rule (that is, one which specifies the penalty for the breach), then not to impose the penalty is another breach. This holds whether the set of rules consists of the criminal law or merely the rules of the family or some other social group, or of an organization. It does not matter that the penalizing rule may have been drawn up with instrumental aims in mind, if the feeling is that it should be followed *because it is a rule*. This account of desert not only provides it with a logical basis: it also offers a psychological explanation of the way in which the rule-following animal reacts to rule-breaking. It may be less inspiring than some other accounts; but it is less metaphorical and more consistent with the facts.

What has to be recognized, however, is that not all penalizing rules are prescriptive. In many penal codes they are: the penalty to be applied is specified, and any exceptions are clearly defined. Even Anglo-American codes have examples of prescription: British examples are the death penalty for treason, the life sentence for murder, and disqualification for certain traffic offences or sequences thereof. Many jurisdictions have prescriptive sentences for a wider range of offences. But when the penalizing rule is permissive, not prescriptive, and does not *require* that a penalty be imposed, a sentencer who feels that he is obliged to impose one cannot justify this feeling by citing the permissive rule. He may of course be able to cite some non-statutory rule. In England, although custodial sentences are merely permitted for most kinds of offence, the Court of Appeal has made it clear that for certain kinds, committed in certain circumstances, they *should* be imposed; and in such cases, an English judge or magistrate is following a prescription. In some other cases he could say that he was following the practice of his local bench, or of the judiciary in general. If he cannot cite something like this as a prescriptive authority he must either be applying a private rule of his own, or not be thinking retributively.[6]

v. Commensurability and proportionality

Retributive punishment raises another problem. Since penalties vary in severity there ought to be some reliable way of deciding what degree of severity (what 'quantum of punishment') is appropriate in each case. Modern criminal codes approach the problem by subdividing law-breaking. They have lists of offences which are defined by the harm done, and in some cases subdivided according to the state of mind of the doer, for example by distinguishing intention, recklessness, and carelessness. Prescriptive codes then lay down the appropriate penalty, with or without modifications to take account of mitigating and aggravating considerations. Permissive codes specify the maximum term of imprisonment or amount of fine, and sometimes the minimum, allowing the sentencer discretion within those limits.

Whether it is the legislature or the sentencer who effectively determines the quantum of the penalty, it is always possible to ask how it is calculated. Why, in England, is the maximum term for theft ten years, but for cruelty to a child, by a person having a financial interest in his care, three years? One kind of answer to such a question is historical and sociological: that the level of penalties reflected the views of legislators and pressure groups at the various times when the legislation was enacted. Yet the fact that penalties for different offences can be, and are, criticized as anomalous points to the need for a different sort of answer: one which will *justify* the quantum. Is death, or life, or seven years, the *right* penalty for a 'gang rape'? Should the fine for driving without due care and attention be £100, or £200, or—in more sophisticated systems—one-tenth or one-fifth of the driver's monthly income?

Legislators and sentencers used to—sometimes still—see themselves as trying to determine the quantum which is 'commensurate' with the harm intended or risked. If they are more sophisticated 'commensurability' also involves adjustment to take into account not only the degree of culpability imputed to the offender but also the degree of suffering, hardship, or inconvenience which a person of his or her sex, age, economic position, social standing,[7] health, or career prospects will experience as a result of the penalty which is contemplated. The calculation is so complex and subjective that only the Recording Angel could safely be trusted with it, and nobody knows what notation he uses.

Another awkwardness is the wide divergences in severity between different penal codes. Various jurisdictions allow the death penalty for murder, rape, robbery, illegal distribution of heroin, and crimes against the economy. Others reserve it for offences of a treasonable kind; others have outlawed it. There are even greater variations in the use of custodial sentences, and the lengths of them. If there is an objectively appropriate degree of severity for any sort of offender, not all these codes can have got it right, or anything like right. The most that their legislators can claim—if they are retributivists—is that they have achieved what they believe to be right, or perhaps, if they are democratic, what their constituents believe to be right.

Hegel's solution to this problem has been adopted by some

modern jurists.[8] If commensurability is an unattainable aim, proportionality is not. Legislators and sentencers can at least ensure that the more culpable offenders are punished more severely than the less culpable: that deliberate murder receives a more drastic penalty than careless driving. Some would say 'a *much* more drastic penalty'; but this leads to the question 'How much more?' This is more awkward than it sounds at first, because the calculation of the 'right' *difference* in severity is as difficult as the calculation of the 'right' *degree* of severity. Yet if this trap is avoided proportionality consists merely in a rank order of differing culpabilities, without any attempt to adjust the gaps between them. This would make it easy to regard most penal codes as observing proportionality. It might even be found that most codes have very similar rank orders: only a few put economic offences above murder, for instance. Yet even codes which have the same rank order may differ widely in a very important respect. Not only may one use very severe penalties, another very lenient ones (which is immaterial from the point of view of proportionality); but one may provide only slight differences in severity between each item in its ranking while another provides very wide differences. One may allow life imprisonment for murder, twenty years for manslaughter, and fifteen years for causing death by careless driving, while another sets a maximum of ten years for manslaughter and allows a fine for careless driving even if this has led to fatal injuries. The sort of proportionality which deals only in rank orders hardly seems satisfying; but the sort which stipulates the width of the differences between degrees of severity for different culpabilities needs the Recording Angel just as much as 'commensurability' does.

I have made the best case I can for the retributive sentencer. Even if he falls back on the sort of proportionality which is content with rank ordering of offences and degrees of culpability, and so dodges the problem of commensurability, it is not a very inspiring case. Anti-retributivists will not be converted by it. Retributivists will probably disown it because my explanation of desert as rule-following does not sufficiently dignify what seems to them an intuitively right—perhaps a God-given—principle. Yet it has the merit of providing not only a logical basis but also a psychological explanation for the feeling that it is in some way wrong if wrongdoers are not penalized.

vi. The negative principle

There is more to be said, however, about retributivism. It seems to involve a negative as well as a positive principle about penalizing people. The negative principle is that only those who have broken rules should be punished. To appreciate its full significance, consider two situations:

(*a*) a particularly shocking or alarming crime has been committed. It is probably desirable that *someone* should be convicted and 'dealt with' for it, in order to reassure and deter; but the real perpetrator cannot be identified. A cynical policy would allow *someone* to be arrested, convicted, and penalized. The negative principle says that this is wrong, however beneficial its effects might be.

(*b*) the perpetrator is identified, but escapes beyond the reach of the jurisdiction, say to Brazil. He is known, however, to be fond of his family. A cynical policy would allow hardship or suffering to be inflicted on them in order to persuade him to give himself up, or at least to make him suffer. The negative principle would forbid this because his family are guiltless.

The interesting thing about the negative principle is that it seems to be accepted even by people who reject the rest of retributivism. Even thoroughgoing instrumentalists hesitate to argue that someone should be hanged for every murder in order that there should be fewer murders. The well-known essay by Hart which drew attention to the importance of 'retribution in distribution', as he called it, suggests that even utilitarians must honour it.[9] There might be occasions on which the penalizing of the innocent might avoid worse evils—such as mass lynchings—but a systematic policy of this kind 'would awaken such apprehension and insecurity that any gain . . . would by any utilitarian calculation be offset by the misery caused'. If his argument is accepted the negative principle can be regarded as having a justification which is independent of the rest of retributivism.

Yet it is breached every day. We may reject the idea of penalizing offenders' families in order to make them suffer, or in order to persuade them to return from Brazil or the Costa del Sol; but we do not reject penalties which, though meant only to affect the offender, inevitably entail suffering, hardship, or inconvenience for their families. Custodial and financial penalties often have this effect (supervisory measures seldom do). We salve our consciences in two ways. We point out that if the negative principle were carried to the length of forbidding the penalizing of the guilty when this would make the innocent suffer, too many of the guilty would enjoy impunity. And we do what we can to alleviate the hardships of prisoners' families, by means of social security benefits and voluntary schemes of assistance. Nevertheless, it is impossible to imprison men and women who have families without causing some degree of suffering to their spouses and children; and it is not a satisfactory answer to say 'the blame rests on the offender because he shoud have foreseen this consequence of his offence'. This is simply one example of the problems created by retributive thinking.

vii. Punishment as ritual

There is one other non-instrumental justification for sentencing which is worth a mention. I have already discussed the denunciatory theory that penalties educate people; but there is also a ritual version which does not make this claim. A sentence can be a dramatic condemnation of an offence or an offender even if it has no effect on the attitudes of citizens who might follow that example. Its function might be merely the satisfaction which people get from a well-performed ceremony. A funeral or a memorial service meets a need to signify regret and respect for the deceased. An induction ceremony symbolizes the acquisition of a status in an organization. The sentencing of an offender, on this view, satisfies because it symbolizes disapproval of what he has done. Like a funeral, it may be an ill-attended ceremony or a thronged occasion; but either way its justification is of this sort.

It is not easy to find unambiguous statements of this version of the denunciatory theory, let alone any real discussion of it.[10] Perhaps it seems to come too close to saying that sentencers must, like priests, try to satisfy their congregations. Certainly it has unusual implications. One of these is that if and when a sentence is meant as a ritual condemnation it must be of a nature and severity which will be interpreted in this way by those who attend or read about the ceremony. This implies that it must not conflict with their notions of what the sentence should be: and these notions are usually retributive. Thus the believer in the ritual version, though he need not himself believe in just deserts, must advocate sentences which appeal to those who do. He is like a theologian who tells priests to say whatever will send the mourners away happy.

Another implication is that the sentence need not always be carried out: just often enough to maintain the belief that it will. This is not as heretical as it may seem. The public do not realize how often fines are not enforced (though for less ritual reasons), or how little of a ten-year sentence a robber is likely to serve. Yet some kinds of sentence are almost frankly symbolic. The best example is the English device of the partly suspended prison sentence. The judge pronounces a sentence of, say, eighteen months, because that is normal for the offence; but suspends half of it because that is all that seems necessary for instrumental purposes. The life sentence too meets the ritualist's needs: a life for a life, but without committing the system to keep the offender until he dies. The ritualist can argue that the public's memory is conveniently short, and that they do not read statistics showing the average time in custody of lifers. In short, he can defend great discrepancies between the formality and the reality. It is this which distinguishes him from the retributivist, who is not satisfied unless the 'right' punishment is actually inflicted. The paradox is that ritualism works for an audience which is retributive but unacquainted with reality, but not for the ritualist, who is neither retributive nor unrealistic. Ritual denunciation is a curiously cynical justification.

viii. Eclecticism

In real life almost all Anglo-American sentencers are what I have elsewhere called 'eclectics', sometimes reasoning retributively, sometimes instrumentally. But 'eclectic' means 'taking one's pick', and the ways in which they take their pick differ. Some decide emotionally, and sentence retributively when they are especially outraged by the crime, but in other cases instrumentally. This could be called 'emotional eclecticism'. Eclecticism, however, does not have to be emotional. It can be based on rational rules. The sentencer's policy might be to sentence instrumentally, except in cases in which it seems unlikely that any instrumental aim would be achieved; and in those cases he might sentence retributively. Alternatively, if he believes in the traditional distinction between offences which are *mala in se* ('wrong because wrong') and those which are merely *mala prohibita* ('wrong because prohibited'), he might deal retributively with the former, instrumentally with the latter. These are simply examples of policies which could be regarded as rationally eclectic: there are other possibilities. Eclecticism is almost unavoidable for sentencers, but they are not told—by statutes, case-law, or guidelines—how to practise it rationally.

Eclecticism sometimes takes an artistic form. Sentencing is said to be an art, meaning not that the results are aesthetically pleasing, but something more subtle. What that is seems worth discussing, since it is never clearly stated. At least part of what is meant seems to be that the good sentencer does not learn to be good in the way in which one learns, say, to be a good doctor: by being told—in books or classes—what works and what doesn't. He must of course learn in this way what his powers are; but not how to exercise the choices which his powers allow him, which is where art begins. Artists learn to improve their use of their freedom by working at the same creation, amending or destroying it, until they feel they have got it right. What tells them that they have got it right is either their own satisfaction or the approval of people whose judgement they respect.

Does this apply to sentencers? The sentencing of an individual is not a task at which they can work in this way until they feel they have got it right. Trial and error of this kind is possible only in a series of sentencing transactions, which makes it much harder to make sense of any belief that they have 'got it right'. It would make sense if (*a*) they were sentencing every case with the instrumental aim of minimizing re-offending and (*b*) were given statistical information comparing the outcomes with the reoffending-rate of offenders who had escaped sentence or been sentenced differently. But (*a*) they sometimes sentence with non-instrumental aims; (*b*) even when their aims are instrumental they are not given the necessary information about the outcomes; and if they were they would have to wait years for it. A belief that one has got it right is more plausible if one's aim is just deserts or ritual denunciation: one can 'feel' right away that the offender has got what he deserves, or that the sentence was a fitting climax of the ceremony, as the case may be. If one does not trust one's own judgement one can wait for letters of approval or criticism, addressed to oneself, to the Lord Chancellor, or to newspapers. If no letters appear, one can argue that one must have got it right. If, like many judges, one looks to colleagues rather than the public for approval, one can ask them what they think of the sentence. Occasionally an appellate court tells the sentencer what it thinks. Even so, it is strange to argue that only by waiting for reactions to one's own sentences can one learn what reactions to expect. Relevant case-law is published for the very purpose of enabling sentencers to know the views of their experienced colleagues *before* they sentence.

In short, it is only the sentencer who invariably sentences with the aim of administering just deserts and trusts his own judgement in preference to anyone else's who can claim, like the artist, to know when he has 'got it right'. If so, however, he must be claiming not only to have assessed the offender's culpability correctly but also to be able to predict how much this offender will suffer as a result of the sentence. In other words he must see himself as a combination of the Recording Angel and Tiresias, who 'foresaw and suffered all'.

12
Juveniles and Justice

Juveniles contribute so much to the statistics of crime, and are the subject of so much special penological reasoning, that they need at least a chapter to themselves. The extent of their contribution can be seen from the examples in Table 12.1. Juvenile males—more precisely those who are old enough to be cautioned or prosecuted—account for 12 per cent of the male population of England and Wales who are old enough to be cautioned or prosecuted. Yet except in the case of fraud and forgery they account for a good deal more than that percentage of indictable offences: well over a third in the case of burglaries, thefts, and criminal damage ('vandalism').[1] Two points have to be made,

Table 12.1 Over-representation of young males amongst cautions or successful prosecutions for eight types of offence

(Based on the *Criminal Statistics for England and Wales, 1984*)

Type of offence	Percentage of males cautioned or successfully prosecuted who were	
	juveniles (aged 10–16)	young adults (aged 17–20)
Personal violence	18	29
Sexual	22	20
Burglary	39	31
Robbery	26	33
Theft, handling stolen goods	36	23
Fraud, forgery	6	21
Criminal damage	35	29
Motoring offences	7	23
Percentages of males over the age of criminal liability who were in the age-group	12	8

however. First, that the young adult age-group, which accounts for only 8 per cent of the prosecutable males, makes an even more disproportionate contribution. It is the second half of the teens in which males are most likely to commit the offences that cause concern. The year-groups most prone seem to be the 15-year-olds and the 16-year-olds, who are either just about to leave school or have just done so. The second point is that juveniles' offences do not usually inflict as much harm as do adults', although quite young children have committed murder, derailed trains, burned down schools, and stolen large sums of money.

The volume of literature devoted to them is in proportion to the anxiety they cause, not only to their families but to everyone who worries about the state of society. Juvenile delinquents tend to be seen as destined for a career of crime. 'Even a child is known by his doings', says Proverbs—and labelling theory (for which see 13.iv). In fact most young delinquents cease to appear in court after they enter their twenties. Many factors seem to be responsible for this 'desistance':[2] association with law-abiding adults—especially women—marriage and fatherhood (not necessarily in that order), success in legitimate occupations or recreations, the learning of long-term rationality (see 6.xi).

What does seem to be true is that the earlier the age at which a child falls foul of the law the more likely he is to fall foul when he is an adult, at least so far as violent or acquisitive offences are concerned. Official intervention at an early stage is sometimes blamed for prolonging the period of delinquency, either because a labelled delinquent has to resort to delinquents for companionship, or because he acquires the psychological knack of coping with whatever the law-enforcement system does to him.

i. The age of criminal liability

For what the law can do is nowadays fairly mild, at least when compared with the hangings, deportations, hulks, penitentiaries, and whippings of previous centuries. Even the age at which a child can be officially treated as a law-breaker has been raised from the Roman age of 7 to the English age of 10,[3] and even higher in Continental jurisdictions.[4] In England it is 'conclusively presumed' by statute, so that not even the strongest evidence to the contrary makes any difference, 'that no child under the age of ten years can be guilty of any offence'. This is obviously a legal fiction: most children of 8 or 9 know the rules about stealing, vandalism, or violence, and do not usually break them under the noses of adults. Some of them know the law so well that they claim their immunity when detected. The most that can be said is that *many* do not *always* realize that what they are taking is someone's property, that what they are doing causes damage, or that fighting or bullying each other constitutes an assault; and that children are more impulsive and forgetful of rules than adults when subject to strong temptation or the influence of elders. The rigidity and severity of law-enforcement systems made it desirable—as even the Romans and pre-Norman Britons recognized—to have a rule which saved children from severe official penalties (but not from chastisement by their parents).

The fiction can have strange results. In 1951 the parents of a seven-year-old were charged with receiving from him a tricycle which they knew that he had stolen. (He had also appropriated a fairy-cycle, but that was not involved in the charge.) They were acquitted—and the acquittal was confirmed on appeal—on the ground that their under-age child could not have been guilty of theft.[5] This is a good example of the malfunctioning of a badly formulated rule. All that the medieval jurists meant to do was to protect children from draconian penalties. All that the common law needed to say was that an under-age child must not be penalized. It need not have said that none of his acts could be offences. Unlike the medieval common law, modern statutes make it clear that even over-age children must not be penalized in the same way as adults (see 12.vi). The need for a legal fiction about the guilt of an under-age child seems to have disappeared.

ii. 'Care or control'

A complicating factor is the substantial number of children whose homes are so unsatisfactory that they become the subject of official concern. They may come to official notice as the result of the child's stealing, truanting, or being found wandering. Local authorities' social work departments can place the child's home under supervision or remove the child. They prefer to do these things with the parents' consent; and some parents acknowledge their inability to cope. As a last resort, however, the local authority can ask a juvenile court to make an order giving it the power to intervene in these ways, on the statutory grounds that the juvenile is in need of 'care or control'. The juvenile must be under the age of 17,[6] but there is no minimum age.

iii. Cautioning juveniles

To return to criminal procedure: the most important development of the last quarter of a century has been the development of diversionary measures for young offenders, chiefly in the form of police cautions (see 7.iii). All police forces of course had recognized for a very long time that bringing children to court for trivial offences was usually a waste of time as well as heavy-handed. Courts themselves seemed to discourage it when they merely discharged the child. An unofficial warning on the spot, or a word with the parents, was often the unofficial solution. Eventually the warning became an official procedure, encouraged by the Home Office. The police are allowed to tell juvenile courts when the child they had just found guilty was not a 'first offender' but had already been warned for an offence.[7] Nowadays it is not only a first detection which can lead to a caution: a second or even a third may do so, if the offences are not very serious (but murder, rape, arson, and the like are too serious). The caution is usually administered to both parents and juvenile at a police station; but a few police forces prefer to do it less formally in the home. Some forces couple the caution with a 'juvenile liaison' system which enables them to keep an eye on the juvenile for a period: an expedient which would be regarded as improper in the case of an adult. The cautioning of juveniles is now so frequent that where indictable offences are concerned nine out of ten boys aged 10, and virtually all girls of this age, are cautioned instead of being prosecuted. The percentages decrease in the older age-groups, but even at age 16 fully one in four boys is cautioned, and one in two girls. After that, when the boys and girls officially become adults, the percentages drop sharply. They are committing more or less the same kinds of offence, but their chances of a caution when detected are only about one in twenty, or one in ten for girls.[8]

iv. The trial of juveniles

When a juvenile is tried, it is normally by a juvenile court of magistrates of mixed sexes, specially selected and trained. Only if he is being tried as an accomplice of an adult or young adult, or is charged with a very serious offence, will he be tried in an adults' court. The normal rules of evidence will apply, with one addition if he is under the age of 14. An adult is presumed to know and intend the nature and consequences of a law-breaking act; but a child of triable age—that is, between his tenth and fourteenth birthdays[9]—is presumed not to have this capacity, and the prosecution is supposed to produce evidence that he knew he was doing wrong: for example that he took precautions against detection.[10] In practice, this rule is sometimes observed rather perfunctorily.

v. 'Conviction' of juveniles

Unless a juvenile is found guilty by the Crown Court, that is by a judge and jury, the finding of guilt is not a 'conviction', only a 'finding of guilt'; although if he is found guilty on a later occasion the court can be told the details of the earlier finding.[11] Nor can he be 'sentenced': a summary court can only 'order' certain measures. The objective is to reduce the stigma of the proceedings (see Chapter 13) to the minimum. With the same objective, the public is excluded from juvenile courts; and the news media, although allowed to report the proceedings, commit an offence if they publish anything likely to identify him. But this does not prevent his friends and relatives from knowing what has happened to him. What is more, if he is tried in the Crown Court for a very serious—and probably very stigmatizing—crime, he is protected from public identification only if the judge makes an order to that effect: something which he does not always do. The inconsistency is hard to defend.

vi. Measures for juveniles

Even in countries which retain the death penalty juveniles are not condemned to it. On the other hand for murder or other very serious crimes they can be detained a long time. In Britain they are not sentenced to 'life', but placed at the disposal of the Home Secretary, usually for an indefinite period, spent at first in some juvenile institution but later, if they become adults before release, in a prison. If mentally disordered, they can be disposed of in the same ways as adults (see 7.vi). They cannot be sentenced to imprisonment; but between their fourteenth and seventeenth birthdays they can be sent to 'junior detention centres' for weeks or months (but not years). These places are run by the Prison Department, with brisk and energetic regimes. Unlike a short prison sentence this measure cannot be suspended, an inconsistency which is defended on various grounds. The only plausible one is that a juvenile is less likely than an adult to remember the threat which is hanging over him when he is being tempted, or led by others, to break the law again.

Yet some of the non-custodial steps which a court can take seem to imply the opposite. A juvenile can be discharged absolutely or conditionally: and a conditional discharge is supposed to warn him that he can be sentenced for his offence if he is in trouble again. A deferred 'sentence' is meant to let the court see how he behaves during the next few months. If he can remember this, he could remember that he is under a suspended detention centre order.

Juveniles can be fined—subject to special limits on the amounts—or ordered to pay costs and compensation (the latter without any limit). Payment is enforceable against parents, who no doubt visit their displeasure on their offspring. Another possibility is an order to spend Saturday morning or afternoon at an attendance centre, engaged in some energetic or useful activity: it is often said that this is the measure of choice for obstreperous football fans; but courts seem to prefer more severe measures for them. Community service is a possibility only when the juvenile reaches his sixteenth birthday.

There are two more flexible measures. One—more often used in 'care' proceedings than in criminal proceedings—is a 'care order' which transfers all the parents' rights to the local authority until the juvenile reaches his majority. Until then it is for social workers to decide whether to find the juvenile a foster home, place him in a 'community home', or leave him in his own home under close supervision (a cheap and easy solution which they are accused of taking too often). But care orders are a last resort, for cases in which there is something seriously wrong with the juvenile's home. Much more commonly used for juvenile offenders is a 'supervision order'. This is modelled on the probation order, and if the offender is 14 or older the supervisor is usually a probation officer (if he is younger the supervisor is a local authority social worker). The requirements attached to the order can be more restrictive than those of an adult's probation order: for example the supervisee can be required to stay at home from 6 p.m. until the following morning. The supervisor can also direct the juvenile to 'intermediate treatment'. What this means varies greatly from one area to another. It may involve something very like community service, or legitimate recreations, or more direct attempts at improving character, with or without short periods spent away from home, for example at camps.

vii. *The welfare principle*

When deciding what to do with a juvenile a court is obliged by statute to 'have regard to (his) welfare and . . . in a proper case take steps for removing him from undesirable surroundings and for seeing that proper provision is made for his education and training'. This applies whether the court is a juvenile or adults' court, and whether the juvenile is before it as an offender or for other reasons. It is only a principle, however, and not a rule: it guides the court but does not tie its hands. It does not rule out considerations of deterrence or public safety, although the Court of Appeal has made it clear that deterrence must be carefully weighed in the balance against the rehabilitation of the juvenile. What needs to be realized is that the welfare principle can point in either direction—towards leniency or severity. It may persuade the court to substitute a fine or some other mild measure for a detention centre order if the latter seems likely to be detrimental to the juvenile; but in another case it may lead it to make a care order or a hospital order which will remove him from home for longer than the law would allow if a retributive or deterrent measure were chosen. The justice of this is often questioned, as we shall see in 12.x. On the other hand, the principle does not give the juvenile's welfare the priority over other objectives which it seems to have in jurisdictions of the Continental or Scots kind, where he is dealt with by 'boards' or 'hearings' in proceedings of a non-criminal sort. Common to all systems, nevertheless, is the assumption that removal from home or the environment in which home is situated is sometimes in his long-term interests, however much distress it may cause him at the time. It would be far-fetched to maintain that no homes are so bad as to justify this. We are forced to rely on a working assumption which we know to be false now and then: that between them courts and social workers arrive at humane and reasonable decisions.

viii. Efficacy

Yet the difficulties of assessing the efficacy of courts' measures, which have already been emphasized in the case of adult offenders, are even greater where juveniles are concerned. In the first place, juveniles' offences are not recorded centrally, only locally. Juveniles are more likely than adults to be cautioned, even when they have previous findings of guilt. Follow-ups can of course trace official cautions in local records, but not incidents which have been dealt with unofficially. Adults may, by and large, be more skilful in avoiding identification: but when they are identified, people have less hesitation in reporting them to the police.

There are more important complications. Measures for juvenile offenders vary greatly from one area to another, even when they have the same official name. It is true that even a probation order for an adult varies in its practical consequences; but the variation is even greater where supervision orders for juveniles are concerned. In particular the 'intermediate treatment' which supervision may or may not involve is a protean concept: in one area it may mean leaving home for periods in a camp, in another attending group discussions from home. So one cannot sensibly ask questions about the efficacy of intermediate treatment: only about the efficacy of this or that form of it.

Even that may overlook something important: the influence of individual personalities on teenagers. Both inside and outside institutions there are rare individuals who seem to have a charismatic effect on the values and conduct of their charges. A project which is lucky enough to have one of these people will produce good results so long as he or she is there. When he or she disappears, so does the effect, because the gift is usually incommunicable.

One more problem has to be mentioned. Whatever beneficial influence a person, a regime, or an activity may have had on a teenage delinquent, the effect may not survive exposure to the rigours of real life outside. Teenagers are even more susceptible than adults to the pressures of the family, of friends or enemies, of cults and fashions. An adult can escape these with less difficulty, at least until he is tied down by a family of his own; but for teenagers it is very hard. Even those who run away or join cults are brought back home. To expect a supervisor, a project, or the 'short sharp shock' of a detention centre to counteract a teenager's environment, human or physical, for more than a short period—what might be called 'the afterglow'—is unrealistic. The afterglow can sometimes be detected by a *short* follow-up; but will be lost in a long one. In the case of adults long follow-ups are preferred to short ones, because the search is for long-term effects. With teenagers there is a strong case for short ones. And they must allow for factors which are either absent or less important in the case of an adult: the fate of his associates in lawbreaking, the delinquency of other members of his family, or the continuation or termination of his education, to mention only a few.

That said, it has to be recognized that the crude aggregate statistics of nearly all follow-ups do not suggest that the routine measures which courts can order are very successful. This is hardly surprising. Most of the teenagers with whom they are dealing have already been cautioned or dealt with at earlier court appearances: if they are 'first offenders' it is only in a technical sense. What should not be inferred is that these measures never have beneficial effects. As in the case of adults' sentences it is equally possible—and a good deal more probable—that *all* of them reduce the likelihood of reoffending by *some* of the juveniles to whom they are applied. This is not to deny that in some cases the measure may increase that likelihood, either because the juvenile regards it as derisory, or because it brings him into association with peers who lead him further astray.

ix. *Aims and justifications*

Yet there is enough uncertainty about efficacy to raise questions about the justification for an approach to juvenile offending which sets store by 'welfare' and the 'individualization'[12] of treatment. In a small minority of cases it is clearly in the interests of a juvenile to remove him or her from home. In another small minority the protection of others from really grave harm is a sufficient reason. It is the everyday cases in which the exact nature of the justification is debatable. If the corrective efficacy of the available measures were marked and undeniable, the debate would be short; but it is not. Failing corrective efficacy, the deterrence of other juveniles is sometimes advanced, usually in support of a fairly simple tariff of mild penalties, which would let juveniles know what to expect if they broke the law. The juvenile court system, however, does not lend itself to general deterrence. The news media are allowed to report only that 'a boy' of a certain age was fined (or whatever) for an assault on another unnamed boy; and as a result seldom cover juvenile courts' proceedings. The news of what the court has done is thus confined to the social network to which the juvenile belongs. The effect of this cannot be dismissed as negligible, because it has not been studied by research workers. Even adult networks which include offenders probably get most of their news about sentences in much the same way. On the other hand, it is usually assumed that juveniles are more likely than adults to commit their offences in an impulsive or forgetful state of mind, and are for this reason less susceptible to deterrence; and this may well be so. What is clear is that a system of unpublicized cautions and court appearances seems designed to minimize rather than maximize deterrence.

x. *'Just deserts' for juveniles*

It is partly scepticism about efficacy, partly a dislike of the inconsistencies of individualization, which have stimulated proposals for a tariff that would be *just*, whatever deterrent effect it might or might not have. The essentials of a just tariff in these proposals seem to be

(*a*) that the severity of the penalty or measure should not be disproportionate to the offence. Riding a bicycle without lights should not lead to a supervision order even if the offence reveals parental irresponsibility. 'Occasionalism' (see 7.vii) is more or less ruled out. Some proposals would allow independent intervention by social workers in cases in which the circumstances of the home are deplorable; but this would take place either without a court order or as a result of separate proceedings of a different nature.

(*b*) that the scale of penalties or measures should be applied with as much consistency as possible; that is, with few exceptions. As in the sentencing of adults, mitigating factors— and presumably aggravating factors too—could be taken into account: for example the influence of older children or the juvenile's previous known offences; but not the fact that most of the family were notorious law-breakers. Consistency is something which is understood and accepted even by law-breakers and children, whereas individualization is not.

The emphasis on the need for a degree of consistency which makes the application of the tariff understandable and acceptable to juveniles and their families is an important feature of proposals such as those of Morris *et al.* (1980).[13] It distinguishes them from a simple revival of the notion of retributive desert. 'The aim . . . is to indicate the unacceptability of the child's behaviour and to impose some constraint on the child.' The message is as important as the punishment. A pure, prescriptive retributivist (see 11.iii) is concerned only with ensuring that the offender is dealt with as he deserves; but Morris *et al.* want him to learn from the punishment. This is a variant of the justification which was discussed in 9.xv: a specialized echo, perhaps, of Gross's theory that punishment tells people that they do not break the law with impunity (see 9.xvii). It does not rely on the hope that the punishment will educate others morally: an effect which, as I showed there, is probably negligible. All it claims is that the offender himself is likely to learn from the penalty.[14]

In any case, logic suggests—as it did in the discussion of adults' sentences (see 11.viii)—that the only realistic approach to objectives is one of rational eclecticism. No single justifying aim could conceivably be attainable in every one of the widely different situations with which juvenile courts have to cope: nor would it be even if their jurisdiction were confined to dealing with offenders for offences. The best the court can do is to decide, without too much optimism, what it has some hope of bringing about. It must then decide whether the permissible means of bringing it about will be seen as fair and consistent by the juvenile and his parents (whose views will influence his). If not, only very weighty considerations, such as the safety of the juvenile or, more often, of others, should persuade the court to adopt the measure in question.

xi. Rigidity and innovation

Although 'juvenile justice' is a special area, it is not completely insulated from the rest of the criminal justice system. Not only have many adult offenders experienced their first detection and its consequences while they were juveniles: most police and probation officers, and many prison staff and magistrates, have had to deal with 'young persons' as well as 'young adults' and older adults. It is the law rather than common sense which draws a sharp distinction between an offender of 16 and one of 17. A striking feature of the history of law-enforcement is the number of innovations which were originally seen as suitable only for juveniles, but which eventually percolated, via young adults, into the rest of the system: supervision, diversion, protection from the death penalty, conditional release from custodial measures, the use of social inquiry reports before imposing a first custodial sentence. These are formal examples: the changes in techniques of supervision and in the regimes of custodial institutions have been too varied to describe. Innovation ought of course to be followed by evaluation, and unfortunately sound evaluative research has been rare. Yet nobody wants a system which makes innovation impossible or very difficult. One of the dangers of the 'just deserts' approach to juvenile offenders is that it could crystallize the rules to that extent.

13

Anonymity and Stigma

Whatever the intentions of law-enforcers—instrumental, retributive, or ritual—an almost inevitable consequence of their intervention is stigma. Whether they merely question a suspect, or proceed to arrest or prosecution, he is a marked man, at least in the eyes of those who know him, and in the eyes of a wider public if he figures in the news media. Even if acquitted he may remain an object of suspicion. 'No smoke without fire', says the man in the street. He is not altogether illogical. The accused would not be on trial if there had not been enough evidence against him to make a case. His acquittal may mean no more than the failure of the evidence to satisfy the court 'beyond reasonable doubt', which still leaves room for a high degree of probability. Only a well-established alibi or the conviction of someone else will save him completely from suspicion. Even so, evidence given in court may have publicized aspects of his life which he would otherwise have been allowed to keep private: his extra-marital affair, his homosexuality, his financial instability, or his heavy drinking.

i. Anonymity for the accused

Only in Sweden does the accused seem to be protected from this sort of publicity. The ethical code of the news media does not allow him to be identified unless and until he is convicted; and even then most offenders are not named. The news media in other countries are less ethical. In 1973 New Zealand legislated to protect the accused against identification unless and until he was convicted; but the legislation was so unpopular with the news media and the legal profession that it was repealed a year later. In 1976 the English bill dealing with the procedure in trials for rape, which protected the identity of the complainant, was amended by backbenchers during its passage to extend similar protection to the accused unless and until he was convicted. The provision has operated for ten years without giving rise to any serious problems. Both the New Zealand and the English statutes have been widely misrepresented. They were accused of being contrary to the principle that 'justice must be seen to be done'; but they did not prevent anyone from watching the trial. They were accused of preventing the police from publicly naming people for whom they were hunting; but they did not forbid this so long as the wording of notices did not accuse anyone of a specific crime. In both New Zealand and England the court was given power to allow the public identification of the accused if this seemed in the interests of justice.

ii. Anonymity for juveniles

Paradoxically, penal reformers are more concerned to protect the guilty than the innocent from stigma. They have more or less succeeded where juveniles are concerned. All countries which have special courts for the trial of juveniles forbid the news media to identify them, whether they are acquitted or found guilty. In the USA their criminal records as juveniles are 'sealed' so that they cannot be cited if the juvenile later appears in court as an adult. It is as if he were reincarnated as a young man with a blameless record. In England the rule is less artificial: findings of guilt before the age of 14 cannot be cited after the age of 20. The public are not admitted to juvenile courts. Justice is not seen to be done, but assumed to be. Inconsistently, if the crime of which the child is accused is very serious, he has to be tried in a higher court to which the public are admitted unless the judge excludes them; and the child's anonymity depends on the judge, who may or may not order the news media to respect it. The result in England at least has been that child murderers have been publicly identified—not only at the time of trial but for decades afterwards—while child shop-lifters have been guaranteed anonymity.

iii. The rehabilitation of reputations

A third kind of protection allows the accused to be publicly identified throughout the criminal proceedings but lets him claim a sort of protection at some later date. In England an offender who is granted a discharge or put on probation by the court is officially treated as not having been 'convicted' for any other purpose. He can, for instance, claim to have no convictions when applying for a firearms licence. More important, the conviction of any offender who is sentenced to not more than thirty months' imprisonment becomes 'spent' after what is called 'the rehabilitation period'. This period varies with the sentence, from six months after a discharge to ten years after a sentence of imprisonment of more than six months (but not more than thirty months).[1] Once the conviction is spent he can deny it, and sue for defamation if it is improperly made public. There are exceptions. The conviction can be referred to in subsequent criminal trials if the laws of evidence otherwise allow this. In applications for certain kinds of appointment he must disclose it. It can be disclosed to authorized research workers. Other countries have simpler provisions. In West Germany convictions are in effect spent after five years or ten years, depending on the nature of the offence, not on the nature of the sentence. In Canada and the USA the offender can apply for a 'pardon' which wipes out the conviction;[2] but in most cases his application leads to official inquiries about his conduct and way of life which reveal his past conviction to employers and acquaintances.

iv. Justifying objectives

Although there is no simple solution to the problem, the variations and complications of the expedients which have been tried raise the question 'Exactly what is the objective?' It cannot be to make those who know the offender forget that he has been found guilty: one cannot legislate for amnesia. It is conceivable that a 'pardon' or the 'spending' of a conviction at the end of the rehabilitation period will alter the attitudes of friends and acquaintances. An analogy might be a discharge from bankruptcy. But the real objective must be something different: the concealment of the fact of conviction from a larger public.

But why is this an objective? Are the reasons connected with the justifications for penalties? Certainly 'instrumentalists' can and do justify attempts to limit stigma on the ground that this makes it easier for some offenders to live law-abiding lives. A person who is known to have a conviction involving dishonesty, drugs, violence, or sexual aberration is likely to have less success than others when applying for jobs. He may find—or think he finds—that former friends are no longer friendly, so that he gravitates into the company of people who also have convictions. He may even—according to 'labelling theory'—be so influenced by the label 'thief', 'alcoholic', 'addict', or 'pervert' that he comes to regard himself as unable to resist whatever temptation the label implies. All these effects, if they occur, are undesirable from the point of view of law-enforcement as well as humanity.

Yet the evidence for the claim that it is the labelling consequences of being publicly found guilty which leads to an increased likelihood of further offending is far from convincing. Nearly all the relevant follow-ups have been concerned with teenagers, and while they found that boys who had been found guilty in court were more likely to reoffend than boys whose offences had not led to a court appearance, they were not able to rule out an alternative explanation. This is that most boys who appear in court are dealt with non-custodially, and may well feel that the consequences of detection are less serious than they had feared, whereas boys who have not yet appeared in court have not had their fears reduced in this way.[3] So far as adults are concerned there is even some American evidence which points in the opposite direction. An FBI follow-up of people released from custody in 1963 found *higher* rearrest-rates amongst those who had been released because they had been acquitted or had cases dismissed than amongst those who had been convicted (and incarcerated, fined, or put on probation).[4] Although the data do not seem to have been analysed very thoroughly, a plausible explanation is that an acquittal or dismissal of case gives the offender more confidence in his ability to 'get away with it'. All that can safely be said, however, is that the statistics do not support the theory that public conviction increases the likelihood of further offending *in the aggregate*.

What the instrumentalist must also take into account are the useful functions of stigma. It is a general deterrent. People who are willing to risk the legal consequences of non-stigmatizing offences, such as bad driving, are less willing to risk the disgrace of a conviction for dishonesty. Even teenaged males, when questioned about the consequences of conviction which would worry them, ranked their families' opinion and the shame of a court appearance above the sentence which they would expect.[5]

Stigma can also warn others of what the former offender may do. That is why teachers who have molested children are blacklisted, though discreetly. Men and women who have been convicted of non-sexual violence are slightly, but undeniably, more likely to behave violently again than people who have not. Banks and other organizations which handle large sums of money understandably want to know whether prospective employees have been convicted of financial dishonesty. It is only when the risk is trivial that the instrumentalist can argue that it should be ignored. He should even be prepared to consider measures specifically designed to warn others of the danger represented by certain offenders: for example requiring drivers convicted of careless driving to display a warning plate on their vehicles, like the L-plate carried by learners in Britain.

v. *Stigma and just deserts*

For the retributivist stigma poses an acute moral problem. If he regards the penalty as being more or less what the offender deserves, the addition of stigma cannot be justified retributively, so that unless it has beneficial consequences—such as warning others of a serious danger—it is regrettable, and should be minimized. Yet if he is a sentencer he may reason that stigma is so certain that he should take it into account, and mitigate the sentence accordingly. If so, however, he is trying to weigh something even more imponderable than the hardship imposed by the sentence itself. If—like most sentencers—he decides to ignore it because it is not his business, he is failing to take into account a consequence of conviction which is often more afflictive than the penalty which he *is* imposing. His dilemma could be solved only by ensuring anonymity for those convicted as well as those acquitted.

The ritual punisher, described in 11.vii, has no problem. He can maintain that the trial and sentence are a ceremony which is complete without any of their practical consequences. This makes it *unnecessary* from his point of view, and so morally wrong, that the offender should continue to be identifiable after he has been sentenced. Since the ritualist is not retributively minded he does not regard the offender as 'deserving' stigma.

Retributivists and ritualists should therefore be in favour of eliminating stigma, or at least minimizing it. Instrumentalists should weigh its obviously useful functions—as a warning and deterrent—against what they believe to be its disadvantages from the point of view of the reduction of crime.

14

Criminalizing and Decriminalizing

It is not only penalizing and stigmatizing that seem to need justifying. The same is true of what is called 'criminalizing': an inelegant but convenient term for the bringing of conduct within the scope of the criminal law.

It may seem more than a little artificial to worry about the justification for the inclusion of such actions as murder, rape, or robbery, which have for centuries been crimes in every jurisdiction worth the name. One of the striking features of criminal codes is that in societies with widely differing histories and values the resemblances between their definitions of serious crimes are more extensive than the differences. To some extent this is attributable to the way in which successive empires have inherited, preserved, and spread the principles of Roman law; but history cannot entirely account for it, and there seems to be something about human actions and reactions which promotes rather than undermines the similarity.

Yet even if the similarities are more impressive, the dissimilarities raise interesting issues. What is more, the second half of this century has seen a new phenomenon. The scope of criminal codes has been (and still is) increasing: new offences are being added every year. In the nineteenth century one or two rather unorthodox thinkers—notably John Stuart Mill—had questioned the assumption that legislators were right in using the criminal law so indiscriminately. It was not until after the 1939–45 war, however, that this critical point of view was taken seriously by legislators. In England the issues which brought the controversy into real life were attempted suicide, abortion, and male homosexuality: in the USA they were 'prohibition' and narcotics control.

Once people had been sensitized to the issue they began to debate other prohibitions: euthanasia, obscenity, birth control, artificial insemination, bigamy, sexual intercourse with minors.

A bibliography of decriminalization would give the impression that our civilization is preoccupied by sex and death.

i. Objectives of the criminal law

Is it possible to discuss the proper content of the criminal law in general terms? If the contents of criminal codes are examined with a sociological eye, no fewer than fourteen different objectives can be discerned:

(*a*) the protection of human persons (and to some extent animals also) against intentional violence, cruelty, or unwelcome sexual approaches;

(*b*) the protection of people against some forms of unintended harm (for example from traffic, poisons, infections, radiation);

(*c*) the protection of easily persuadable classes of people (that is, the young or the weak-minded) against the abuse of their persons or property (for example by sexual intercourse or hire-purchase);

(*d*) the prevention of acts which, even if the participants are adult and willing, are regarded as 'unnatural' (for example incest, sodomy, bestiality, drug 'trips');

(*e*) the prevention of acts which, though not included under any of the previous headings, are performed so publicly as to shock other people (for example public nakedness, obscene language, or heterosexual copulation between consenting adults);

(*f*) the discouragement of behaviour which might provoke disorder (such as insulting words at a public meeting);

(*g*) the protection of property against theft, fraud, or damage;

(*h*) the prevention of inconvenience (for example the obstruction of roads by vehicles);

(*i*) the collection of revenue (for example keeping a motor car or television set without a licence);

(*j*) the defence of the State (for example espionage or—in some countries—political criticism);

(*k*) the enforcement of compulsory benevolence (for example the offence of failing to send one's children to school);

(*l*) the protection of social institutions, such as marriage or religious worship (for example by prohibiting bigamy or blasphemy);

(*m*) the prevention of unreasonable discrimination (for example against ethnic groups, religions, the female sex);

(*n*) the enforcement of the processes regarded as essential to these other purposes (for example offences connected with arrest, assisting offenders to escape conviction, and testimony at trials).

These objectives are so diverse that it may seem out of the question to formulate any general principles which will help to decide whether a given sort of behaviour should or should not be treated as a crime. For example, we are several centuries past the era in which the criminal law was thought of simply as the secular institution for the punishment of moral wrongdoing (if indeed this ever was wholly true), and we now recognize that many sorts of conduct which we condemn morally are outside its proper scope, while other sorts within its scope are from the moralist's point of view trivial, neutral, or even defensible.

Does this mean, however, that it is impossible to formulate any rules or principles to which we can appeal if we are asked to decide whether a new crime should be created or an old one abolished? Is the issue to be decided simply by the strength of feeling that can be aroused amongst legislators at an opportune moment? Certainly this is how many such decisions have been taken in this century over the last hundred years. In England the crime of 'gross indecency between males' was created in 1885 by Henry Labouchère, a back-bench member of Parliament who—for some reason which has never been satisfactorily explained—successfully moved this amendment to a bill which was designed to protect immature girls from sexual exploitation. The crime of incest was created in 1908 in response to pressure from the Church of England, which had only recently begun to discover how many slum-dwellers were unaware of the prohibitions of Leviticus. The Litter Act of 1957 was the result of a private member's bill, supported by the Council for the Protection of Rural England. The Hypnotism Act 1952, which prohibits stage hypnotists from using subjects under the age of 21, was the result of a single unfortunate incident in the Brighton Hippodrome.

It is easy by examples such as these to discredit our present method of drawing and redrawing the boundaries of criminal law. Is it possible to improve on it?

ii. Moral limits

Now and again there have been attempts to formulate what might be called 'limiting principles', which declare that the criminal law should *not* be used for certain purposes, or in certain circumstances.

The oldest seems to be

(A) Prohibitions should not be included in the criminal law for the sole purpose of ensuring that breaches of them are visited with retributive punishment.

It is not too far-fetched to ascribe this principle to Beccaria, whose *Of Crimes and Punishments* (1764) was the first treatise on penal theory to deal with the subject on utilitarian premises.[1] His assertion that 'It is better to prevent crimes than to punish them. This is the ultimate end of all good legislation' is the assumption with which the approaches of all later utilitarians, such as Bentham, Mill, and Baroness Wootton, begin.

Some years later, Bentham's *An Introduction to the Principles of Morals and Legislation* (1789) stated three more limiting principles. The first was

(B) The criminal law should not be used to penalize behaviour which does no harm.

In his phraseology, punishment was groundless when, on the whole, there was no evil in the act. It is a principle to which everyone would give general assent, and would agree that it was the reason why we do not use the law to discourage bad manners or bad art. Nevertheless there would be many disagreements over other sorts of conduct. The idea of prohibiting bad art by law sounds ridiculous, but one of the things which town and country planning legislation tries to control is bad architecture, and anyone who flouts it can suffer heavy penalties.

Another of Bentham's principles was

(C) The criminal law should not be used to achieve a purpose which can be achieved as effectively at less cost in suffering.

For instance, suggested Bentham, if the objective could be achieved 'by instruction . . . as well as by terror', terror should not be used. The trouble about this principle is that Bentham talks as if deterrence and instruction were interchangeable so far as everyone in a given category is concerned. He may simply have meant, of course, to exempt from punishment very young offenders who needed only to be warned that what they had done was a crime. But if he meant, as he probably did, to exclude whole classes of harmful conduct from the criminal law, he overlooked the possibility that some of the people who indulge in such conduct might respond to deterrence but not instruction. A better formulation of the principle would be

(CC) The criminal law should not be used where measures involving less suffering are as effective or almost as effective in reducing the frequency of the conduct in question.

Bentham's third principle was

(D) The criminal law should not be used if the harm done by the penalty is greater than the harm done by the offence.

For in such cases punishment would be 'unprofitable' when the felicific balance sheet was added up. The difficulty about this principle is that it requires us to weigh, let us say, the unhappiness caused by bad architecture against the unhappiness caused by a large fine. Since the two sorts of unhappiness are inflicted on different people we cannot simply leave it to individual choice, as we do when we ask someone whether he would rather be fined or pull his new house down. The difficulty of choosing between incommensurables is one of the weaknesses of Benthamism which have been exploited by its opponents.

A variant of this principle, however, seems to underlie a modern argument that has been used against the wholesale prohibition of abortion or homosexual acts. It has been pointed out that such sweeping laws give rise to practices which, on any point of view, are more undesirable than those against which they are aimed. When legal abortions are difficult to arrange, the result is a black market in illegal ones, with its high mortality. The outlawing of private homosexual behaviour between consenting men provided excellent opportunities for blackmail. The undiscriminating prosecution of bigamists must have endangered many unions between men and women which, though unhallowed, were stable and happy.[2] If Bentham had written today his comment would probably have been that

(DD) The criminal law should not include prohibitions whose by-products are more harmful than the conduct which they are intended to discourage.

Unfortunately this involves the same difficulty as principle (D), although to a lesser degree. For principle (DD) is of help only when the prohibited conduct is so clearly less harmful than the by-products of the prohibition that there can be little disagreement on the subject. It is not surprising, therefore, to find that principle (DD) is invoked only when the conduct under discussion is of a kind which makes it possible to maintain either that the harm which it does is illusory or negligible, or that it harms only the person who indulges in it. It has been argued, for example, that marijuana-smoking in moderation is not in itself harmful to the body or mind, and that what does harm is the black market, created by the prohibition, which leads marijuana-smokers to associate with criminals, and especially with sellers of 'hard' drugs.

Others would argue that even if drug use is harmful—and there can be little doubt that some drugs are destructive—they harm only the user, who has freely chosen to use them (often, it is added, as an escape from some other kind of misery). Bentham himself recognized the existence of what he called 'self-regarding offences', which harmed only the offender, and which he thought it 'inexpedient' to punish. It was Mill, however, who developed this into a full-blown principle:

The object of this Essay is to assert only one very simple principle, as entitled to govern absolutely the dealings of society with the individual in the way of compulsion and control, whether the means used by physical force in the form of legal penalties or the moral coercion of public opinion. That principle is that the sole end for which mankind are warranted, individually or collectively, in interfering with the liberty of action of any of their number, is self-protection. The only purpose for which power can be rightfully exercised over any member of a civilized community, against his will, is to prevent harm to others. His own good, either physical or moral, is not a sufficient warrant.[3]

Leaving aside, for the moment, the fact that Mill was talking about other forms of coercion as well as the law, a modern statement of his assertion might be this:

(E) The criminal law should not be used for the purpose of compelling people to act in their own best interests.

Mill himself recognized that there should be exceptions to this rule. 'Despotism', he thought, 'is a legitimate mode of government in dealing with barbarians provided that the end be their improvement'; and he took much the same view of the upbringing of children. So far as children were concerned, therefore, he would not have said that his principle ruled out compulsory benevolence such as enforced attendance at school.

What he himself had in mind were 'infringements of liberty' such as legal restrictions on the sale of poisons, on drunkenness unaccompanied by violence, on gambling, and on Sunday amusements. He was not concerned with the question whether these were morally wrong or not; he was arguing that even if they were wrong nobody should attempt to use the law—or indeed the pressure of public opinion—to discourage others from such behaviour, since it did no harm to anyone except possibly the drug addict, the drinker, or the gambler himself. Other would-be reformers of the law have of course gone further, and argued that some of the acts which the law prohibits on the assumption that they are morally wrong are not wrong at all, or wrong only in special circumstances. Suicide, euthanasia, gambling, drinking, drug-taking, abortion, and private homosexual behaviour have all been defended in this way. If their defenders had used Bentham's language they would have said that in such cases punishment is 'groundless'. For Mill, however, this was not the point. Whether such behaviour was wrong or not, the law should not be used against it.

Mill's principle has gained wide support in this country over the last century, probably because of its emotional appeal to a freedom-loving intelligentsia rather than the strength of the reasoning on which it was based. He himself thought that the strongest argument for it was that although an 'over-ruling majority' were likely to be right more often than not about the conduct that affected the interests of other people, when it came to 'self-regarding conduct' they were quite as likely to be wrong as right: and he cited a number of obviously ridiculous discrepancies between the moral beliefs of different religions and cultures. He seems to imply, however, that if a majority were in fact in the right they would be justified in interfering with self-regarding conduct. A stronger argument would have been that the object of such interference is usually to force people to behave morally, but that—as Herbert Hart has pointed out[4]—there is no virtue in morality if it is imposed from without.

Mill also had to meet the counter-argument that many of the types of behaviour which he wished to protect against interference were not, in the long run, self-regarding after all. As our subsequent experience has emphasized, the drinker, the drug-user, and the gambler are likely to cause suffering to their dependants, relatives, and friends and to become eventually a burden which society has to carry. Mill's answer was rather forced and moralistic:

. . . I cannot consent to argue the point as if society had no means of bringing its weaker members up to its ordinary standard of rational conduct, except waiting till they do something irrational and then punishing them, legally or morally, for it. Society has had absolute power over them during all the early portion of their existence; it has had the whole period of childhood and nonage in which to try whether it could make them capable of rational conduct in life.[5]

If (he is saying) society has failed to take its opportunity of ensuring that their upbringing protects them against the temptations of drink, drugs, and gambling, it should not try to remedy its failures by punishing them when they are adults.

The argument is at once Utopian, perfectionist, and penologically out of date. Utopian because it assumes that society can control the upbringing of children and teenagers to this extent. Perfectionist because it asserts that if one has failed to achieve something desirable in the best possible way one should not be allowed to try the next best: an odd principle. Penologically out of date because it overlooks the possibility that the law might be a means—perhaps the only means—of compelling the alcoholic, the drug addict, or the gambler to undergo therapeutic treatment. Mill himself was writing in an era of deterrent penal measures, and could hardly be expected to envisage this.

iii. *Pragmatic limits*

The principles which Beccaria, Bentham, and Mill formulated were moral prescriptions, which said that the penal system *ought* not to attempt this or that task. Other writers, however, were pursuing a more pragmatic line of thought and asking what the law could reasonably be expected to achieve. This is how Montesquieu approached the subject in *The Spirit of the Laws*[6]. He recognized that prohibition by law can be carried further in some societies than in others, but thought that in any kind of society there were areas of conduct (which he called 'les mœurs et les manières') in which it was most unwise to use the law in the hope of effecting changes.

Even Mill's most violent opponent, the Victorian judge James Fitzjames Stephen, accepted pragmatic limits of this sort to the interference of the criminal law. In *Liberty, Equality, Fraternity*,[7] which was a bitter attack on Mill's essay, he admitted that 'you cannot punish anything which public opinion, as expressed in the common practice of society, does not strenuously and unequivocally condemn. To try to do so is a sure way to produce gross hypocrisy and furious reaction.'

In the less emotional language of the twentieth century this principle might read

(F) The criminal law should not include prohibitions which do not have strong public support.

The principle has its own weaknesses—such as the difficulty of measuring public opinion in a morally pluralistic society. Like Mill's principle its justification is not self-evident, and it raises the question 'Why not?' Stephen's own reason seems to have been 'because of the gross hypocrisy and furious reaction which would result if one failed to observe this principle'.

Whether Stephen could have supported his argument with convincing examples is doubtful: certainly subsequent experience suggests that he overstated it. Our attempts to improve people's driving of motor cars by means of the criminal law have certainly been made without the 'strenuous and unequivocal condemnation' of public opinion. True, each successive attempt to strengthen penalties or improve means of enforcing the law has met with organized opposition from the motorists' associations. Admittedly some of their arguments might fairly have been regarded by Stephen as 'gross hypocrisy': but not as the 'furious reaction' that he predicted.

The importance of Stephen's principle, however, lies in its recognition that there are practical limits to the scope of the criminal law. Bentham and Mill wrote as if there were no difficulty in detecting and punishing any sort of offence, even self-regarding ones; and their principles were moral prescriptions. Punishment ought not to be inflicted if it is groundless, needless, unprofitable, or inefficacious, said Bentham; self-regarding offences ought not to be discouraged by law or any other form of coercion, thought Mill. Stephen, who was a lawyer and a judge, lifted the problem out of the armchair of moral philosophy and into the slightly fresher air of practical politics. The fact that he was arguing in favour of punishing many offences which Mill would have exempted from the criminal law makes him, by modern standards, reactionary; but it does not mean that all he said should be disregarded.

On the contrary, it is worth asking in the light of modern experience 'What are the practical, as distinct from the moral, considerations that suggest limits to the scope of criminal law?'

An obvious practical consideration is the economics of enforcement. The chief agencies of enforcement are police forces, whose size is restricted by the amount of public money which the society in question is willing to spend on them. Even if this were not a limiting factor, it would be found that the number of suitable men and women willing to be recruited to the police was not large enough to make an enormous expansion possible. Allocating policemen's time to the best advantage will always be a major problem, but the extent to which it regulates the rigour of law-enforcement is not fully appreciated. In many cities a report of a theft involving property of less than a certain amount is not even passed to the detective branch for fear of wasting their time.

Another important consideration is the law-enforcement agencies' need for the assistance of the private citizen. Apart from a selection of driving and parking offences, of revenue offences, and breaches of health or safety regulations which can be detected and brought home to the offenders entirely by the observation and evidence of the police, inspectors, and other officials, very few offences would come to official knowledge if they were not reported by private citizens (see 14.i), and very few of these would be traced to their perpetrators if it were not for the information which the police are able to obtain from the same source.

There are some offences, indeed, which could seldom be prosecuted without the evidence of one of the participators. One of the reasons why women who have resorted to criminal abortionists are so seldom prosecuted in England is that their evidence is usually needed to secure the conviction of the abortionists. Again, most police forces are so determined to convict blackmailers that they will refrain from prosecuting the victims who give evidence against them. One of the dangers inherent in the extension of the criminal law to a multitude of peccadilloes is that by making a larger percentage of the population into targets for law-enforcement agencies it may forfeit the co-operation of this percentage in the enforcement of the more important prohibitions. An obvious example of this possibility is traffic offences, which now account for the great majority of all convictions. It is impossible to assess the amount of co-operation which the law-enforcement agencies forfeit by such prosecutions, but it must be considerable. The same is true of prosecutions for possession of marijuana.

Even when prosecutors could secure convictions without too much trouble they often refrain from doing so in cases where they believe that strict enforcement would alienate the public. In England, youths who can be proved to have had sexual intercourse with girls not far below the statutory age of consent (at present 16) are often not prosecuted, largely because the police feel that public opinion would not support them. Another rather unpopular indictment is bigamy, which in England is not prosecuted nowadays unless there is evidence that the guilty party went through the form of marriage in order to deceive the other party into having sexual intercourse or into parting with property. In countries where private homosexual behaviour between consenting adult men is still criminal, prosecutions for this are often restricted to cases in which there is evidence or suspicion of proselytizing, commercial exploitation, blackmail, or 'orgies'.

Another assumption which seems to underlie some arguments against certain prohibitions is that

(G) A prohibition should not be included in the criminal law if it is unenforceable.

The word 'unenforceable', however, is used very loosely in such arguments. Does it mean 'such that *some* breaches of it would not be detected'? Hardly, for in this sense every prohibition is unenforceable. Does it mean 'such that *all* breaches of it would be undetected'? Again, hardly; for it is no easier to think of any prohibition that would be unenforceable by this criterion. Perhaps the nearest thing to a genuinely unenforceable prohibition in the history of English law was the form of treason which consisted of 'imagining' the death of the king, the queen, or the heir apparent, before it became established by case-law that an overtly treasonable act must be proved. What the principle must mean is that

(GG) A prohibition should not be included in the criminal code if only a small percentage of infringements of it could be proved against the infringers.

In this form the principle at once raises the question 'How small must the percentage be?', which is impossible to answer precisely, and not at all easy to answer even roughly until some reply has been given to the more fundamental question 'Why is relative unenforceability an argument against the inclusion of the prohibition?' The stock answer to this is that it 'brings the law into disrepute'.

Like so many stock answers this needs a very close examination. It can hardly mean that a complete absence of attempts to enforce a particular law discredits the whole criminal code, or law-enforcement agencies in general; for the history of every criminal code has plenty of instances in which prohibitions have been allowed to fall into desuetude, without any evidence that this weakened respect for the operative parts of the code. Does it mean that the agencies of law-enforcement make themselves ridiculous by unsuccessful attempts to secure convictions? If so, this could be remedied very easily by taking action only when the prospects of succeeding are very good, as the police do with speeding offences.

A more plausible form of the argument might be that if those who are prosecuted for a given offence are regarded by their fellow citizens as a small and unlucky selection from those who actually committed it, the public may come to feel that their prosecution is 'unfair'. That such a feeling might well be irrational—especially if the offenders knew that they were risking prosecution—would not prevent it from being widespread. Certainly offenders who are unlucky enough to be prosecuted for a commonly undetected offence—such as exceeding speed limits—seem to feel it.

At most, however, this would be an argument for extreme caution in actually prosecuting detected breaches of the prohibition, and not an argument against including the prohibition in the criminal code. For quite a strong argument can be put forward for retaining, or indeed inserting, even unenforceable prohibitions. The argument is that the law influences conduct not merely because people are deterred by the possible consequences of infringing it, but also because it is taken as a declaration of what the society in question condemns. This theory—which I have elsewhere called 'the declaratory theory'—resembles the denunciatory justification of penalties (see 9.xv), but is distinguishable because it asserts that even if no one were ever penalized for a breach of a prohibition (indeed even if no one knew what the penalty was) it would still help to maintain standards of conduct.

Certainly the clearest examples of the use of this argument have been connected with prohibitions whose enforceability was doubtful at the very best. It was put forward to the Wolfenden Committee on Homosexual Offences and Prostitution by witnesses who were against the relaxation of the law on homosexual acts between men; and the sole member of the Committee who dissented from this relaxation expressed the objection by saying that 'Many citizens . . . regard the prohibitions expressly imposed by law as the utmost limit set to their activities . . . and the removal of the present prohibition from the criminal code will be regarded as condoning or licensing licentiousness.'[8] At least one Home Secretary has used the argument to defend legislation which was avowedly designed to influence opinion rather than penalize conduct. During the second reading of the Race Relations Bill of 1968 Mr Callaghan said: 'I attach great importance to the declaratory nature of the first part of the Bill. I believe that . . . the very process of giving the law brings an instinctive response from the great majority of our citizens.'[9]

Whatever one's views on these particular laws may be, the argument is not implausible. We know that in other areas of opinion, such as politics, people are apt to alter their judgements to correspond with what they believe to be the view of the majority. Experiments in which I collaborated with Leonard Berkowitz confirm that university students' views on the morality of certain actions can be strongly influenced by telling them the results of fictitious opinion-surveys of their peers.[10] Might not the criminal law function as a powerful means of inducing people to believe that a given type of conduct is strongly condemned by their peers?

In the experiment students at two universities were asked to rate the moral wrongness of actions such as being drunk (but not disorderly) in a public place, and not trying to stop a person who is seen to be attempting suicide. In the second stage some of the students were told of the moral views of 'over 80 per cent of students' in a recent (fictitious) national survey, while other students were told that the acts or omissions described had recently become 'legally permissible' or 'illegal', as the case might be: a control group were simply given the same items to rate again without any new information of either kind. Both the information about the 'national survey' and the information about the changes in the law produced changes in students' moral ratings, of the predictable sort; but the most marked changes were produced by the 'survey' information. These results support the hypothesis that knowledge of the legality or illegality of conduct influences moral attitudes to that conduct. A similar finding was a by-product of the experiment by Mrs Marsh and myself, described in 9.xv. It was conducted at a time when the wearing of seat-belts in the front seats of cars was not compulsory, but was about to be made so. The parents who were interviewed were told this, and asked how much they would disapprove of not wearing a seat-belt (a) 'at the moment' and (b) 'when it becomes an offence'. Their ratings were markedly higher for (b).[11]

iv. A positive justification?

The thoroughgoing pragmatist, however, is one who abandons the defensive approach. Instead of merely setting up warning notices in the form of limiting principles which try—not very practically—to indicate to legislators where they should stop, he asks why the onus of proof should not lie on those who want to extend the scope of the criminal law. They should, on this view, be required to show why it is desirable. Shifting the burden of proof in this way has obvious difficulties. The very diversity of functions to which I have already drawn attention makes any attempt to approach the problem in this way sound naïve. Nevertheless, if an institution is as costly—whether in terms of economic resources or of human happiness—as the penal system undoubtedly is, it seems more realistic to ask for positive justifications whenever it is to be used against a given sort of conduct.

If possible, these justifications should not appeal to moral sentiments of the sort that condemn certain kinds of behaviour. They should not assert that the criminal code should prohibit this or that because it is wicked. To assert this is to invite argument as to what is or is not wicked, and in any society—let alone one which contains so wide a diversity of moral views as Britain—areas of disagreement will quickly be found.

Something like a non-moralistic justification was offered by Sir Patrick (now Lord) Devlin, in his well-known lecture on *The Enforcement of Morals*, where he said

The State must justify in some other way [than by reference to the moral law] the punishment which it imposes on wrongdoers and a function for the criminal law independent of morals must be found. This is not difficult to do. The smooth functioning of society and the preservation of order require that a number of activities should be regulated.[12]

It was unfortunate that the main purpose of his lecture was to examine the Wolfenden Committee's recommendation that homosexual acts in private between consenting adults should not be criminal. For it led him to argue, in effect, that private homosexual acts between men might well arouse such 'general abhorrence' that they did in fact threaten our society with disintegration. This was so obviously unrelated to the social and political facts that—together with other weaknesses in his argument—it laid him open to attacks from Hart and other spiritual descendants of Mill.

Nevertheless, the misapplication of a principle does not necessarily invalidate it; and, however injudiciously, Devlin was in fact stating one of the main axioms of a philosophy which seems to underlie a good deal of modern penal legislation. The need to ensure 'the smooth functioning of society' must, after all, be the main justification for the parts of the criminal code which are concerned with the protection of health, the collection of revenue, and the defence of the realm—objectives (b), (i), and (j) in my list. Most, though probably not all, of the other prohibitions can be regarded as necessary for 'the preservation of order', to the extent at least that if they were not enforced on some occasions there would be disorder. Not all thefts or damage would provoke public disturbances; some victims, for example, would be afraid to retaliate. But some would not, and their methods of protecting themselves or avenging their losses would lead to breaches of the peace. The same is true of intentional violence against the person or unwelcome sexual advances. The prohibition of these can be justified because they are classes of actions of which by no means all, but a substantial number, would provoke disorder.

Nevertheless, there are some prohibitions which it is not very plausible to justify in this way. The obvious examples are in my group (d), which consists largely of sexual behaviour that has come to be regarded as 'unnatural', and is prohibited by many criminal codes even if it takes place in private, and between participants who are adult, sane, and under no coercion or inducement other than their own desires. (It is interesting to note how difficult it is to think of any form of non-sexual behaviour that is regarded as so 'unnatural' as to call for the intervention of the criminal law. Coprophagy, for instance, strikes an enormous majority of people as unnatural, but is not prohibited in any criminal code of which I know.) So long as sexual acts are genuinely private, and do not involve advertisement, coercion, deceit, or the persuasion of the young or mentally disordered, they are most unlikely to provoke disorder.

The difficulty of arguing, however, that such prohibitions are in the interests of public order or the smooth functioning of society is not an argument for seeking some other kind of justification. For it is just this sort of prohibition about which modern legislatures are uneasy. In the minority of civilized societies in which the criminal code still prohibits homosexual behaviour between consenting adult males, the prohibition seems to be enforced with less and less enthusiasm or efficiency, and its justification is questioned with increasing frequency.

At first sight there is another category of penal legislation which is not easy to justify on Devlin's principle: what I have called 'compulsory benevolence'. It is implausible to argue that the evasion of universal education or national schemes of social insurance is likely to lead to breaches of the peace. It is not so unrealistic, however, to suggest that children who are allowed to grow up illiterate or more than usually ignorant in a technological society, or people who make no provision for sickness or old age, become economic burdens on their society, and perhaps nuisances of other kinds. This being so, compulsory benevolence can fairly be said to be in the interests of the 'smooth functioning' of society.

It must be admitted that instead of attempting, like Mill, to draw an eternal boundary between what may and what may not properly be regulated by official sanctions Devlin offers only a shifting frontier. What may provoke disorder in one generation or one society may not do so in a more tolerant one. In a society which is thrown into a panic by rumours of witchcraft it may be desirable—in a peace-keeping sense—to prohibit witchcraft, as administrators have found in Africa. This does not mean, of course, that the prohibitions should be enforced by medieval penalties. What it does mean is that those who see no harm in witchcraft must make some progress in communicating their enlightened viewpoint to the society in question before demanding the abolition of the law that prohibits it.

Without discussing all the frontiers of the criminal code in detail, I have tried to show that it is not out of the question to formulate both limiting principles and positive justifications which are considerably less dependent on moralistic assumptions and values than, for example, Mill's principles. It is true that they are no more precise. There is just as much room for argument about what is necessary for the smooth functioning of society or the preservation of order as there is over the question of what is or is not a purely self-regarding offence. But whereas arguments over self-regarding offences are apt to end in deadlock between two or more moral viewpoints, disputes as to what is or is not detrimental to smooth functioning or order do allow for some sort of appeal to observable fact and experience.

Can it be argued, however, that the demand for a positive justification based on the smooth functioning of society and the preservation of order is completely value-free? In the first place, it assumes that the society in question is one that *should* be allowed to function in an orderly way. Some people regard some societies as so iniquitous or inequitable as to make this a misguided objective. This can be conceded, however, without surrendering the whole approach. It is quite consistent to hold that for those who believe in a given sort of society a sensible objective of the criminal law is to promote its orderly functioning, but that for those who object to that kind of society disobedience is a rational technique for changing it. If we regard the criminal law as simply an instrument designed for this limited purpose, both the values of the society which it serves and the values of the enemies of that type of society are outside the scope of this particular argument. This does not imply that those who breach the criminal law in attempts to change or overthrow a society have a claim to be exempt from its penalties. It is possible to argue that the penalties are excessive, or even—if one is so minded—that political motives should be a mitigating circumstance when people kill or rob, without holding that deliberate homicide or robbery should not be crimes.[13]

v. *Pragmatism versus morality*

One interesting feature distinguishes the pragmatist's approach which I have just been discussing from the moralist's approach. Suppose that both are agreed in disapproving very strongly of some type of conduct. For the pragmatist the question is simply whether on balance anything useful would be achieved by invoking the criminal law against it. The moralist, however, seems to agonize in a special way over this step. He may be willing to see all sorts of other steps taken to reduce the frequency of the conduct—education, propaganda, restriction of opportunities— and yet may consider it morally wrong to use the criminal law in the campaign.

It is hard to see, however, what it is that in the moralist's eyes distinguishes the criminal law. It may of course be simply that he regards its penalties as excessively severe; but that is not an essential feature of the criminal law. Would he still object if a fine were the maximum penalty for whatever conduct is in question? He might still object that the criminal law seeks to *compel* whereas other techniques of social control work by persuasion or indoctrination. This seems an undeniable distinction, which appeals to one's instinctive dislike of being ordered to do something, even if it is in one's interests.

It raises two questions, however. Are all other techniques of social control less objectionable morally than the compulsion of the criminal law? Is one-sided indoctrination—for example against birth control or abortion—any better? The second question is whether a strong and sincere belief in the harmfulness—or sinfulness—of the conduct does or does not create a duty to do what one can to prevent it, short of doing even greater harm. Whether or not one takes sides on this issue, it is clear that the moralist has a choice between three positions, two simple and one complex:

(*a*) he may hold sincere and well-defined views about the wrongness of conduct and yet think it wrong to try to influence the behaviour of others by *any* means (a very rare position);

(*b*) he may on the other hand think it justifiable, even

obligatory, to seek to influence the behaviour of others by *any* means (a fairly rare position);

(*c*) he may take position (*b*) with a difference, regarding *some* means as unacceptable (the commonest position of the moralist).

Note that (*c*) involves ruling out certain *means*, not certain types of conduct. The difficulties for the moralist of drawing distinctions between types of conduct which he may or must seek to eliminate and those which he should not have already been shown to be insuperable, if not in theory, at least in practice. It is the techniques about which he has to worry. So far as the use of the criminal law is concerned, he has to decide whether, with all its crudities and undesirable side-effects, it is less acceptable than, say, one-sided moral indoctrination.

15

Victims and Victimology

Criminology has been criticized for being more interested in the offender than in his victim. Law-enforcement is open to the same stricture. In primitive societies, lacking an authoritative agency of law-enforcement, the victim or his family had great influence on what happened to offenders, or at least those offenders who were not so powerful as to be immune from retaliation. It was the victim who accused the wrongdoer and the victim who accepted compensation or, failing that, mustered enough armed friends to retaliate. 'Buy off the spear or bear it' was the Saxon saying. It was when feudal superiors took over the responsibility for peace-keeping that certain forms of wrong became matters for independent adjudication and punishment, processes in which the victim was merely the accuser, and the penalty benefited nobody except the law-enforcer. It is only in the modern period—the last two centuries—that legislatures have begun to reinstate the victim in the criminal process, and allow him to put his claims for redress before the sentencers.

i. Victims as initiators of law-enforcement

Yet in spite of the way in which the law has shouldered the victim aside, there is one foothold which it has never been able to deny him. Most offences would not come to official notice if ordinary people did not report them. Some kinds, it is true, are observed by police vigilance, or as a result of 'proactive' policing which does not merely react to reports but sets out to 'catch offenders at it'. Examples are speed traps on highways, plain-clothes detectives in public lavatories or football crowds, and 'stings' in which government agents pretend to be dealers in stolen goods or drugs. It is only a minority of prosecutions, however, which result from such enterprises. Much more often it is the people who are harmed, frightened, outraged, or inconvenienced by offences who invoke the agencies of the law.

Even so, victims are selective. As we have seen (in 3.iii), there are many offences which they do not report. The reasons are extremely varied:

(*a*) those who know about the incident may not realize that it could be regarded as an offence. Children do not think in this way when they are abused by adults, hit by friends, or have their property taken by force. We have seen that some offenders, too, are unaware that what they are doing falls within a defining rule of the criminal law.

(*b*) some incidents are seen as breaches of non-criminal codes rather than the criminal law, and are dealt with accordingly. Minor violence on the football field is penalized by the referee, even when it could be prosecuted as an assault.

(*c*) the 'victim' may be a willing participant in the offence, as under-age victims of sexual offences sometimes are. Witnesses, too, may enjoy what they are watching, whether it is sexual activity, cock-fighting, or fouling at rugby.

(*d*) a victim may be unwilling, or a witness disapproving, and yet reluctant to complain because he or she does not want the offender to suffer the official consequences. This is one of the reasons why some sexual offences are not reported, but it also operates in the case of petty thefts, drunken driving, and many other offences.

(*e*) a victim or a witness may be too afraid of reprisals. It is not only terrorists who inspire fear of this sort: gangs of children in housing estates can make life anxious for neighbours who complain to the police about them. Employers think twice before reporting thefts by staff, in case the result is 'industrial action'.

(*f*) reporting may seem simply too much trouble. Dangerous driving goes unreported because motorists cannot be bothered to stop and telephone the police. Customers who see others shoplifting do not want to 'get involved'. Getting involved may mean more than simply finding a shop assistant, or telephoning the police. It may lead to the taking of statements, and to appearances in court which are bound to be inconvenient and may turn out, under cross-examination, to be traumatic.

(*g*) the victim or witness may dislike the police so much that he will have nothing to do with them, even when he has no need to fear that they will charge him with any offence. His dislike may be the result of past dealings with them, or merely reflect the attitudes of his family or neighbours.

(*h*) the victim or witness may realize that reporting will draw attention to his own role in the transaction. Obvious examples are blackmailers' targets; prostitutes' clients who find their wallets gone; illegal gamblers who find that the game is crooked. Slightly different is the situation in which the victim or witness has played a completely innocent part in the incident itself, but is involved in other illegal activities which might come to light as a result of official attention. An employer may decide not to report an embezzling member of his staff because his accounts would reveal tax-evasion.

(*i*) it may seem unlikely that the police—or any official agency—could do anything effective if the incident were reported. Many people realize how low the chances are of recovering money or goods which are stolen from cloakrooms, changing-rooms, unlocked cars, or railway carriages. Realism apart, however, some people believe that the police are uninterested in some kinds of offence (such as driving offences which result in no injury or damage), while others believe that it is difficult to interest them in offences committed in troublesome areas, unless they are of a very serious kind.

(*j*) the harm done by the offence may seem too trivial. The stolen property may not be worth much. The assault may have caused little or no injury. The indecent exposure may not have frightened the victim. Misuse of the company's telephones or other facilities may be accepted as endemic, and as a small price to pay for good relations with staff.

(*k*) the victim or witness may disapprove of the law which treats the incident as an offence. Examples are poaching, illegal abortions, homosexual acts, prostitution, euthanasia.

In some jurisdictions a person who knows of but fails to report the commission of a serious offence is himself guilty of an offence. In England it used to be possible to charge him with 'compounding a felony'; but in 1967 this was removed from the criminal code, and a person can now be charged only if he has in some way conspired with, or helped, an offender either to commit an offence or to escape justice.

Thanks to surveys of potential victims we now know a little about the relative frequencies with which these reasons for non-reporting operate. Victim surveys do not always subdivide these reasons in the way in which I have done; and in any case they can hardly be expected to identify examples of reasoning such as (*a*), (*c*), or (*g*). Children are not usually questioned, and there are other categories which are not usually interviewed: the homeless, hospital patients, members of the armed forces, people who spend most of their evenings at work or in bars. With these reservations, however, the tabulation which resulted from the British Crime Survey of 1981 is interesting:

As we have already seen (in 3.iii) the frequency of non-reporting is especially high in the case of 'personal offences': thefts from the person (mostly pocket-picking), assaults, robberies, sexual offences. Table 15.1 shows that even in such cases by far the commonest reason was the triviality of the harm done

Table 15.1 Reasons why the police were not notified

Question: 'Did the police come to know about the matter?' If 'no', 'Why not?' (Multiple answers allowed)

	Personal offences %	Household offences %
Too trivial; no loss or damage	38	49
Police could do nothing	16	34
Inappropriate for police; dealt with matter ourselves	13	5
Fear/dislike of the police	6	1
Inconvenient	5	2
Police would not be interested	3	9
Fear of reprisals	2	<1
Reported to other authorities	3	2
Other specific answers; vague answers	21	10

(and that it was even commoner for 'household offences': vandalism, burglary, and so forth). Two other reasons were fairly common: that the police could do nothing, and that it would have been 'inappropriate'—however the respondent actually put it—to involve them. Fear or dislike of the police was a minor but not insignificant reason when the offence was personal, but much less frequent when it was a mere household offence: this may be associated with the sorts of people who are most often the victims of violence.

ii. The chances of becoming a victim

Nearly every adult takes some sort of precaution against some sorts of crime. He may not carry a weapon or a personal alarm; but he probably locks his car when he parks it, and almost certainly locks up his home when he leaves it. Older people are careful where and when they go out, and whom they let through their front doors. For some people the fear of being burgled, mugged, or otherwise molested is enough to affect the quality of their lives. Yet until recently it was only insurance companies which took an interest in the actuarial probabilities of victimization amongst their insurers. Even so, their statistics are of value only to them, because people who insure themselves or their property against crime are not representative of the population as a whole, or even of those who are old or have been victimized: only of those who can afford the necessary premiums and have the necessary providence.

Better information has been provided by victim surveys. Table 15.2 is based on the 1981 British Crime Survey.

Surveys of this kind usually also question respondents about their fears of being victimized. In the case of some kinds of crime it seems to be those who are least likely to suffer who are most afraid. Table 15.3, also taken from the 1981 British Crime Survey, illustrates this.

Clearly it was the older respondents who were most apprehensive about, but at the same time least likely to become victims of, 'street crime'. The explanation is partly that a lifetime of exposure to news media which selectively report the mugging and molesting of the elderly has exaggerated their estimates of the

Table 15.2 Offences in England and Wales, 1981: British Crime Survey estimates

Household offences	Rate per 10,000 households
1. Vandalism	1,494 ± 182
2. Theft from motor vehicle	700 ± 88
3. Burglary[a]	410 ± 70
4. Theft of motor vehicle[c]	156 ± 34
5. Bicycle theft	118 ± 24
6. Theft in a dwelling	78 ± 36
7. Other household theft[a]	835 ± 114

Personal offences	Rate per 10,000 people aged 16 +
8. Common assault[a]	396 ± 94
9. Theft from the person[a]	112 ± 32
10. Wounding	98 ± 34
11. Robbery[a]	42 ± 28
12. Sexual offences[ab]	16 ± 10
13. Other personal theft[a]	413 ± 64

a. Categories 3, 7, 8, 9, 11, 12, and 13 include attempts.
b. Only women were asked about sexual offences; rates are per 10,000 females.
c. Most of the cases of theft of motor vehicles involved unauthorized taking (where the vehicle was recovered). It is sometimes more useful to express rates for vehicle offences on the base of vehicle-owning households. The best estimate of the rate for theft of vehicles is 232 and for theft from vehicles, 1,040. The rate of cycle theft among households with cycles is 287.

Table 15.3 Fears for personal safety after dark and risks of 'street crime'.

Question: 'How safe do you feel walking alone in this area after dark?'

		% feeling 'very unsafe'	% victims of 'street crime'
Men	16–30	1	7.7
	31–60	2	1.6
	61 +	9	0.6
Women	16–30	15	2.8
	31–60	17	1.4
	61 +	34	1.2

frequency of these incidents, but it is partly also that the consequences of being attacked are genuinely more likely to be serious when the victims are elderly.

Probabilities are often overestimated: yet this does not always mean that they are unrealistically related to actual probabilities. When the crime in question is burglary, for example, it seems that fear of it is in fact commoner in areas where burglary is commoner, as Table 15.4 (this time from the 1983 British Crime Survey) demonstrates.

As for violence, some potential victims are well aware that they run higher-than-average risks, even if they over-estimate them.

Table 15.4 Burglary risks and fears, by neighbourhood groups, 1983

	Households burgled (including attempts) in 1983	'Very worried about burglary'
	%	%
Low-risk areas		
A. Agricultural areas (n = 476)	1	10
C. Older housing of intermediate status (n = 2,001)	2	18
K. Better-off retirement areas (n = 463)	3	17
J. Affluent suburban housing (n = 1,659)	3	18
B. Modern family housing: higher incomes (n = 1,537)	3	20
Medium-risk areas		
E. Better-off council estates (n = 1,018)	4	25
D. Poor-quality older terraced housing (n = 759)	4	29
F. Less well-off council estates (n = 1,175)	4	31
High-risk areas		
I. High status non-family areas (n = 609)	10	25
H. Multiracial areas (n = 400)	10	36
G. Poorest council estates (n = 543)	12	41
National average	4	23

Young blacks in the cities of the USA often carry weapons, for homicide is the most frequent cause of death for this demographic group. Homicide is less common in Britain, but in some city areas young men are so often attacked that weapon-carrying is almost excusable. Some occupations carry high risks: the police, security guards, counter-staff of social security offices, prostitutes, to name only a few, are well aware of this. There are high-risk recreations too: gambling, hitch-hiking, visiting night-clubs.

By contrast, there are groups of people who are unaware of their danger. Tourists do not realize that their dress and leisurely comportment marks them out as targets for muggers, especially if they are obviously foreigners. But the most important example is children. In England—and probably elsewhere—the first year of life is the time when one's chances of dying from intentional violence are highest; and the most likely killer is one's mother. At the age of 5 one enters a safe period, when one's chances are only about two per million. After that they are about eleven per million, although for women they are slightly lower. About non-fatal violence to children we have much less accurate information. Nowadays doctors and social workers are fairly alert to identify 'at risk' children, the usual signs being bruises, fractures, and obvious fear of a parent. Even so too many children who have suffered violence from parents are allowed to remain with them, or if removed are returned to their homes by over-optimistic social workers.

iii. Victim-precipitation

Von Hentig, the German criminologist who first drew attention to high-risk groups, also pointed out that some people would not have become victims if they had not behaved as they did. The notion of 'victim-precipitation' was popularized by Wolfgang (1958), with his convincing examples of homicides for which the slain seemed almost as responsible as the slayer. Some had started the fight that ended in their deaths: some were spouses or lovers whose cruelty or provocation drove their partners to violence. Other victimologists have described ways in which victims of sexual offences contribute to them by conduct, dress, manner-isms, or conversation that seem to invite sexual advances.[1] It is unfortunate that excessive use of this excuse by some sexual offenders has provoked equally excessive denials by feminists. Less controversial are blackmailers, who would not be in business if nobody behaved disreputably. Black-marketeers—especially of currencies—are dependent upon customers who want to take illegal advantages.

Less obvious are the cases in which it is luck rather than justice which labels A as the offender and B as the victim. B may have started the fight, but suffered worse injuries, so that he ends up in hospital and A in court. If two under-age youngsters have sexual intercourse, it is the boy who is much more likely to be charged or cautioned, whatever part the girl played. The assumption seems to be that he is either the initiator or the partner who had the more self-control.

Even when there is no doubt about who is the victim and who the offender, the notion of victim-precipitation is extremely elastic, as some examples will show:

(*a*) V accepts a challenge to a fist-fight, but in the fight O uses a knife;

(*b*) V engages in conduct which he knows to infuriate O, not seeking violence but overestimating O's self-control;

(*c*) V ventures without protection into a district which he or she knows to have a high rate of violent crime, without a compelling reason for doing so, and is mugged by O;

(*d*) V agrees to sexual intercourse with O, but withdraws consent during the preliminaries;

(*e*) V intentionally stimulates O's sexual desire, but refuses to satisfy it;

(*f*) V dresses so as to enhance her sexual attraction, but without intending to attract O specifically: he commits an indecent assault on her;

(*g*) V invites O to take part in an illegal transaction, such as a currency offence, and is cheated by O;

(*h*) V purchases goods or services offered by O at a price which V knows to be exceptionally low, and is cheated by O;

(*i*) V leaves his car unlocked for a few minutes while making a telephone call, and O steals it;

(*j*) V, a shopkeeper, deliberately makes his counters attractive to children, and leaves them unsupervised. O, a child, steals from V's shop.

It is not surprising that different researchers, using different criteria, arrive at widely varying estimates of the percentages of homicides, rapes, and robberies which are victim-precipitated.[2] These estimates are very relevant to crime prevention (the subject of Chapter 16), especially when they enable policy-makers to tell potential victims that by doing this or avoiding that they can greatly reduce their chances of being the victims of whatever sort of crime they fear. But an inference of a more debatable kind is sometimes drawn from them: that the offender's culpability is lessened because his or her victim behaved as he or she did. A common example is the claim that supermarkets, by encouraging shoppers to feel the need of goods which they can remove from the counter, diminish the responsibility of those who intentionally avoid paying for them. Sexual offences committed by men against women who have voluntarily associated with them are the subject of similar inferences. But there is a risk of fallacies. One is to reason that because the victim has behaved carelessly or against advice, and therefore deserves some degree of censure, the offender deserves a reduced degree of censure. The conclusion is justified only if the result of the victim's behaviour is to subject the offender to temptation, provocation, or misapprehension of a kind which to some extent excuses his offence. A victim who merely makes himself an accessible 'target' for the offence is 'responsible' for it merely in a causal, not a moral, sense. He is responsible in a moral sense only if he does something which he knows to be likely to incite the offender to commit the offence.

Even when this fallacy is avoided confusions can arise. In 1983 an English judge had to sentence a car-driver who had raped a hitch-hiker. The judge referred to her behaviour in hitch-hiking at that time of night as 'contributory negligence' and reduced what would normally have been a stiff prison sentence to a fine of £2,000. The first point that needs to be made is that the concept of contributory negligence belongs to the civil law, not the criminal law. More important, even in civil law a defendant who has *deliberately* caused harm is not normally held less culpable because the other party has acted negligently. In a later case the Lord Chief Justice made it clear that imprudent behaviour on the part of a rape victim is not a mitigating factor where the offender is concerned, unless it led him to believe that she would consent to intercourse.[3] Rape is not the only offence in which such confusions are encouraged by defence counsel. When employees embezzle some of the money they have to handle it is often urged by way of mitigation that their employer's lax system made this temptingly easy.

Outside court, the same confusions may affect the attitude of the man in the street either to an individual offender or to a whole category. They may lead to generalizations of the kind which claim that shop-lifters are partly excusable because stores make their merchandise so attractive and accessible; or that driving at 100 miles an hour is the fault not of the driver but of manufacturers who make a selling point out of the speeds of which their cars are capable. Moralizing on these lines is not a complete waste of time. It can lead to political pressure for measures that are more effective than law-enforcement: for instance limitations on the performances of motor vehicles. What it does not justify is the illogical conclusion that shop-lifters or fast drivers are rendered incapable of resisting temptations simply because they are in the shop or in the driving seat.

What needs scientific study—and has begun to receive it—is the way in which people are influenced when apportioning blame. What psychologists call 'attribution theory' throws light on this. Although attribution theorists have devoted more attention to inferences about causal responsibility, a few studies have been concerned with moral responsibility. Jones and Aronson (1973) found that Texas undergraduates attributed more 'fault' to victims of rape who were married or virgin than to those who were divorcees, even when the circumstances described were otherwise identical.[4] Yet interestingly, they did not recommend shorter sentences for men who raped married women or virgins. Perhaps they made the distinction I have been making, between censuring victims for exposing themselves to victimization and excusing those who took advantage. Attribution studies, however, would be even more relevant if they could tell us how jurors, magistrates, and judges reason when they apportion blame between victims and victimizers.

iv. Reparation[5]

Independent of these developments in knowledge and theory about victimization has been a revival of interest in the notion of reparation: of ensuring that victims receive some benefit by way of redress for the injury, loss, damage, or distress which they have sustained. Primitive systems of law attached more importance to this than to penalties. It lost this importance when criminal law was clearly distinguished from civil law, and it was found expedient to fine, kill, banish, or imprison those whose behaviour threatened 'the peace'; but the civil law continued, in theory at least, to recognize victims' claims to compensation. In practice, civil litigation has always been too expensive and cumbersome for the typical victim; and in any case there is little point in establishing a claim against an offender who is dead, in prison, has no money, or has fled abroad.

Most of the more affluent countries—following the lead of New Zealand—have therefore established systems for compensating victims out of public funds. Virtually all, however, limit their scope to victims of personal violence: to compensate victims for loss of property would be far too costly even for prosperous economies. Other limitations are also common. Victims whose own conduct seems to have contributed to the violence are excluded. So are claims for small amounts (and in some countries quite large ones). Some schemes exclude claims from foreigners, or from people who have suffered at the hands of a close relative, although the logic of this is hard to follow. When compensation is allowed, it usually covers medical or funeral costs, and loss of earnings due to the injury. In Britain, and a few other North American states, it can cover shock and distress. The victim must have reported the crime to the police within a reasonable time, and must have co-operated in the investigation of it.[6]

The victim who is excluded from compensation by the state can seek it from the offender in the courts—if he knows who the offender is. An increasing number of jurisdictions allow him to present his claim to the criminal court which is dealing with the case. By no means all victims, however, are told of their right to do this; and some are not even told when the offender is due to appear in court. When a claim is made, this is usually done at the sentencing stage. English criminal courts like to have clear, undisputed evidence of what is due, and are apt to take the line that controversial claims are for the civil courts, however unrealistic this is.[7] Even when they make awards, by way of compensation orders, these are usually small in comparison with the awards of civil courts or of the State's Criminal Injuries Compensation Board. But there are two good reasons for this. One is that most of the injury claims in court are for injuries so minor that they are excluded from the scope of the State scheme. The other—which applies to claims for both injuries and property—is that the offender seldom has the money with which to meet a large claim in full. The English rule of practice is not to order him to pay more than he can afford by way of instalments spread over twelve months. If he also gets a prison sentence this is likely to be a negligible sum. A sentencer will therefore sometimes avoid, or suspend, a prison sentence so as to make it possible for the offender to go on earning; but the propriety of this is questionable. Should an offender escape a prison sentence simply because he is lucky enough to have a job and to have inflicted harm that calls for compensation? Should a comparable offender go to prison because his blow missed, or the goods were recovered, or he had no hope of paying? The dilemma is sharpest for the retributivist who believes in equal punishment for equal culpability.

At present, criminal courts do not, on the whole, refrain from imprisonment with the sole object of enabling the offender to pay compensation. The need to punish, deter, or protect is seen as overriding this objective. By way of contrast, if the appropriate penalty is a fine sentencers are very willing to reduce the amount of this in order to enable the offender to compensate. English sentencing law expressly gives compensation preference over the fine. Paradoxically, an offender who is let off with a police caution (see 7.ii) or otherwise diverted from prosecution cannot be ordered by a court to compensate. He may well have offered—even paid—compensation in order to persuade the police or the prosecutor that he is a suitable case for 'diversion'; but he cannot be made subject to a compensation order without being convicted. Since 'diverted' offenders have admitted their guilt this curious exemption is hard to defend.

The problems encountered by all systems for compelling offenders to compensate are the poor financial position of most of them; the difficulties of extracting money by instalments from unwilling payers—who may even disappear; and victims' ignorance of the procedure for making claims (unless the victim is needed as a witness he may not even be told whether, when, or where the offender is coming to trial).

v. The victim's needs

For those, however, who attach most importance to the victim's feelings the payment of compensation, however inadequate, is the aim that should have priority. Victims are said to get more satisfaction if compensation is paid by the offender than if it is paid by the State, probably for retributive reasons.[8]

Compensation may not be the victim's only need. If the crime was one of violence or sexual molestation there is more urgency about medical treatment, and in some cases psychological help. Medical treatment usually takes priority, even over the understandable desire of the police to get statements and other kinds of evidence from the victim. Psychological help seems to be regarded as less urgent, and is usually left to relatives. In recent years, however, victims' need for professional help has been recognized, especially in cases of rape and incest. 'Rape Crisis Centres' have been set up in many large cities, to deal not only with the immediate psychological aftermath but also with the long-term effects—anxiety, depression, fear of men—which may be lasting handicaps. There are also, in some cities, organized groups which offer help to victims of other disturbing offences, such as non-sexual violence and household burglaries. Unlike schemes of compensation from public funds, these are provided by local, voluntary efforts. Even where this help is available, however, many victims are not told of it; and some of those who are prefer privacy or the comfort which relatives or psychiatrists can provide.

vi. Mediation

Interest in reparation has recently developed into efforts to 'mediate' between victims and offenders.[9] The occasional success of efforts at 'conciliation' between parties in divorce suits has encouraged the hope that similar attempts might succeed where offences of a not too serious nature are involved. Usually 'mediation' is confined to cases in which it has been decided not to charge the offender but to 'divert' him (see 7.xi). If mediation were attempted while the offender was awaiting or undergoing trial or sentencing it might improperly affect the evidence given on either side, and might in any case put the offender in a position in which he felt obliged to make concessions which he privately considered to be unjust. Mediators want concessions by either side to be voluntary.

Their aims are mixed. Sometimes it is the victim's state of mind which is intended to benefit, by the reduction of resentment, desire for revenge, or anxiety about the possibility of suffering further offences. Sometimes it is the offender's attitude, either to the individual victim or to victimizing vulnerable people, which is the target. The hope is that by seeing and listening to his victim he will better appreciate the extent of the harm he has inflicted.[10] In cases in which the offender and the victim are likely to continue to have contacts with each other—for example when the offence consists of domestic violence—the intention is also to improve relations between them. It is too early, as yet, to look for scientific assessments of the extent to which these aims are being achieved. Techniques for managing the negotiations between the parties are still the subject of trial and error. It is very difficult for mediators to combine an appearance of impartiality with other functions. If one of the parties, for instance, is much less articulate or forceful than the other it may be necessary to support him or her in the discussions; but interventions of this kind may convince the other party that the mediator is taking sides. If the negotiations are unsuccessful the result may be that both parties feel unjustly dealt with. Even an agreed compromise which satisfies the mediator may leave both parties disgruntled. The only benefit that can so far be hoped for with any confidence is the lightening of the workload of the summary courts, by providing an alternative to formal proceedings where minor offences are concerned; and mediation is not yet common enough to have a substantial effect of this kind.

Mediation schemes are organized not by the State but by local agencies, usually of a voluntary kind, although in England probation departments have played a part. They are encouraged, however, by the responsible ministries, chiefly in the hope that some day they will make a substantial contribution to the diversion of cases from the courts. If this hope is fulfilled, the victim will owe his reinstatement not to justice but to economy.

16

Preventing and Fighting

The pessimism of recent years about the efficacy of measures directed at offenders, identified or potential, coupled with scruples about incapacitation, selective or unselective, has intensified interest in prevention. The approach is not new. Generations of locksmiths have made a living out of it. But it is only in the last decade or two that real scientific invention has been applied to the problem, and that some criminologists have made a speciality out of the theory and evaluation of preventive strategies.

'Crime-prevention' can be used in a fairly strict sense so as to denote only measures intended to make the commission of some sort of crime, such as burglary, impossible or at least so difficult that potential offenders are discouraged. Usually, however, the term is also used to refer to devices or expedients which, while not making the crime more difficult, increase the likelihood of detection: burglar alarms are the obvious example. Some criminologists use it so as to include devices which make it easier to undo the harm caused by a crime, an example being the marking of valuable articles with post-codes so that if stolen they can be identified. Some books on prevention even discuss measures of social welfare which are meant to reduce the numbers of people who are motivated to commit crimes. There is no convincing evidence that they have this effect: the case for welfare measures rests more firmly on other foundations, and they are outside the scope of this chapter (but see 7.i).

The preventive approach, however, makes hard-headed sense, at least where property is concerned. In most societies it is no longer realistic to believe that only a small percentage of the population are ready to take advantage of opportunities to steal, embezzle, defraud, pilfer, or vandalize, or to imagine that they are easy to identify, still less that they can be discouraged or reformed by means that most societies are prepared to tolerate. The property which we want to protect, on the other hand, is easily identifiable, and we have a considerable degree of control over its whereabouts, its visibility, and the ease with which it can be stolen or damaged, even if we do not always think it worth the trouble to make use of that control.

i. Displacement

Critics of preventive approaches, however, point out that protecting property of this or that sort against theft or vandalism may achieve a success which is, in a sense, illusory. The property in question may be stolen or damaged less often, but at the expense of other sorts of goods to which the thieves or vandals are diverted. 'Displacement'—to use the technical term—has certainly been shown to take place. In 1971, when steering-column locks became a standard fitting in all new British cars, thefts of new cars in London decreased by about two-thirds, but thefts of old cars nearly doubled; and in New York a police 'crack-down' on subway robberies seems to have been followed by an increase in street robberies.[1] These are merely examples in which the researchers who were evaluating the effects were able to find obvious targets to which the crimes in question were likely to be displaced. More often the displacement is likely to be diffused rather than focused on targets where it can be measured. Even if it could be shown that the prevention of robberies or burglaries in one location was not followed by an increase in the same type of crime in other locations, the possibility of displacement has not been ruled out. Frustrated robbers may resort to burglary, and vice versa. Only in an ideal situation, in which it is possible to be sure that all offences of dishonest acquisition are reported, could researchers be expected to do the necessary counting. In real life it is next to impossible to show that displacement has *not* taken place.

Yet even if a certain amount of it is likely, it is not a very convincing objection to a policy of encouraging prevention. It is true that everyone who protects himself or herself against dishonest offences very slightly increases the risks run by people who are less well protected. It is also undeniable that some of these other people have more difficulty in taking precautions, whether because of the nature of their occupations, the areas in which they live, or their inability to afford protective devices. But this line of argument leads to the conclusion that people in such situations should be selectively assisted to protect themselves, not that more fortunate people should take no precautions. Examples of selective assistance are the special minibus services which some agencies provide for people who have to travel home from work through high-risk streets.

ii. Protecting persons

Even without that sort of assistance people can be given useful advice which, if taken, will lessen their risks of being mugged or otherwise molested while they are outside their homes. When it is dark they can avoid unlit or ill-lit open spaces, or make sure that they traverse them in the company of others. Empty bus stations, underground platforms, railway carriages, public lavatories, and even, in some buildings, elevators should be avoided. People can equip themselves with personal alarms. The carrying of weapons, such as knives or tear-gas sprays, is illegal in most jurisdictions, although in some a woman or elderly person who is found to be armed in this way is unlikely to be prosecuted. Children can be warned—by parents or teachers—not to approach car-drivers who stop to speak to them, and to have nothing to do with strangers who try to engage them in any activity. School and playground staffs should be on the watch for men who hang around without children of their own. Young children should be escorted to and from schools and other meeting-places.

The harm done by violent people can be reduced by depriving them of the most deadly kinds of weapon. Firearms control in the UK probably helps to keep the murder-rate below that of the USA, where a far larger percentage of the population is allowed to possess hand-guns. In Britain it seems to be easier for robbers to arm themselves with sawn-off shot-guns, although control of a sort is exercised over possession of shot-guns, and it is an offence to shorten their barrels. More commonly, it is knives rather than firearms which are used in fights and hold-ups. In the UK it is an offence to carry an offensive weapon in a public place without lawful authority or reasonable excuse; and a knife suitable for stabbing is undoubtedly an offensive weapon. In certain contexts, such as riots, courts may even decide that an empty bottle or a bicycle-chain comes within the meaning of this undefined term. Other jurisdictions prefer to specify what may not be carried in public: for example knives with blades more than four inches long. The point of such prohibitions is not merely that the lack of a gun or a knife will make it less likely that the victim will be seriously injured: it will often mean that no violence at all takes place. Another kind of weapon is broken glass, which can inflict nasty injuries when a smashed bottle or tumbler is thrust into the face, as often happens in bars. For this reason some bars use paper cups instead of glasses when they are expecting trouble. If someone invented a type of glass that did not form sharp edges when smashed, and was inexpensive enough for use in bars, he would be popular in casualty departments. Meanwhile this is a preventable hazard which we do not prevent. A fourth kind of weapon which is popular is heavy footwear. Some young men are distinguishable by boots with heavy soles and reinforced toe-caps, admirably adapted for kicking a fallen victim. Whether such boots are 'offensive weapons'—in UK terms—is not clear.

iii. Protecting homes

Most householders nowadays pay attention to their door-locks and window-fastenings; and there is a flourishing market for these devices, as well as for burglar alarms. Interviews with British burglars, however, have shown that when selecting 'targets' what they pay attention to are signs that occupants are at home; the presence of dogs; access to the rears of houses; and shelter from observation while they are breaking in.[2] It is only when they have approached the house that the degree of security provided by locks and window-fastenings may discourage them. An important precaution is therefore the avoidance of any indication that the home is unoccupied: for example uncollected milk-bottles or mail, drawn curtains during daylight hours, absence of lights at night, uncut lawns. Householders should also be suspicious of callers who say they are looking for someone who lives in the neighbourhood, or for a straying cat or dog. Telephone callers who do not identify themselves may also be finding out whether the occupants are at home (answering machines tell them that the home is unoccupied for considerable periods). Women who live alone should not advertise that fact by their entries in telephone directories.

iv. Property marking

Even property which is difficult to protect can be made easier to recover if it is marked in such a way that the owner can be identified. Arrests of professional burglars often reveal large collections of valuable goods awaiting disposal for which the original owners cannot be traced. The remedy is indelible or invisible marking with the owner's individual post-code. In Britain most car-dealers are willing to engrave registration numbers on car-windows, so that a change of number-plate is a risky trick. The knowledge (or belief) that property is identifiable sometimes contributes to prevention by deterring thieves.

v. Protecting cash

Most thieves, robbers, and burglars prefer cash to saleable property, although some teenagers steal radios, cassette-players, and similar expensive things for their own use. People who are known to keep or carry large amounts of cash are tempting targets. Credit cards[3] and cheque-books can make this unnecessary for most people; but there are occupations in which real money is essential. Keepers of small shops have to hold considerable amounts of it, and are especially vulnerable when they walk to deposit it at a bank. Cashiers at lonely all-night petrol stations are often robbed. Taxi-cab drivers are another attractive target; and in some cities they carry escorts in the front seat and have strengthened glass between them and their customers.

The ordinary citizen, however, can do quite a lot to protect whatever cash he has to keep at home or carry with him. There are small safes which can be bedded unobtrusively in a wall or floor (other hiding-places are usually familiar to experienced burglars). Money carried on the person is safer in a pocket than in a wallet or handbag, and the pocket should have a zip-fastener. Money-belts are safer still, but so inconvenient and uncomfortable that they are used only by those who travel rough.

vi. *Protecting neighbourhoods*

It is not only individual homes that can be made safer; neighbourhoods can. Unplanned or badly planned developments start at a disadvantage. Narrow lanes between windowless walls or high hedges; pedestrian tunnels under highways; raised walkways against the upper floors of shops or flats; secluded rear-access paths behind houses: all these make molestation or burglary easier than they need be. Even a neighbourhood with these handicaps, however, can be made somewhat safer by conscious vigilance. Inhabitants of rural homes have an eye for strangers—or neighbours—who approach their homes or buildings; and urban dwellers too can be made aware of the value of this. Organized vigilance is still better. 'Neighbourhood watch' schemes are promoted by many police forces. A reliable citizen acts as a liaison officer between the police and local residents, who are encouraged to tell him of any suspicious happenings, or strangers who are observed in their area, so that he can relay the information to the police. To what extent this reduces the frequency of common crimes, and to what extent it merely displaces them, is a question to which the answer must vary from one district to another; but even displacement benefits the vigilant. Vigilance must of course be distinguished from 'vigilantism'—patrolling by self-recruited posses who carry out their own arrests, and even sometimes their own punishments. This is strongly disapproved by law-enforcement agencies, even when it seems successful, because of the risks, injustices, and barbarities which it sometimes involves. Neighbourhood watching, on the other hand, has no such dangers, for watchers or suspects; it provides a useful pastime for retired or unemployed citizens, and is good for the morale of a community.

vii. *Protecting road-users*

Unlike city planners, designers of roads have paid a great deal of attention to ways of minimizing victimization. Most of the ingenuity has been devoted to preventing collisions between vehicles or overturning on bends; but some designs have had the pedestrian in mind. Traffic islands are sanctuaries. Underpasses were meant as safe conducts, but are apt to conceal muggers at quiet times of day: foot-bridges are safer. The speeds of vehicles can be kept down by 'sleeping policemen'—deliberately constructed humps or undulations in the road surface. In the 1939–45 war mechanical governors were fitted to some military vehicles, chiefly to reduce petrol consumption: but the idea is being revived as a means of preventing excessive speeds.

Since drunken driving is a major hazard, there have been efforts to make it harder for drunks to get their vehicles in motion. One device presents the driver with a display of random numbers, which he has to register in reverse order before the ignition key will work. Unfortunately it is an expensive accessory which alcoholic drivers are unlikely to instal without compulsion. Something more ingenious is needed. As for careless drivers, a less expensive accessory, which would warn other road-users that they were within range of a hazard, would be a red H-plate. Drivers convicted of careless driving could be required to display this for a period after their conviction, just as holders of provisional licences are required to display L-plates. The stigma of an H-plate would also be a deterrent.

viii. Making precautions compulsory

There are a few kinds of crime against which precautions are required by law in some jurisdictions. In Britain firearms must be locked up when not in use. Explosives, too, must be stored in lockfast buildings, although these are often in deserted places where it is easy to break in unobserved. In some West German towns by-laws make it a finable offence to leave a parked car unlocked. Legal requirements of this kind are often criticized on the ground that people should be free to choose the degree of risk they run; but this argument is short-sighted. It is obviously myopic when the risk is the theft of a firearm or explosive which will probably be used to commit a serious crime against someone else. Even an owner who leaves his car unlocked because he personally is not very worried about it or its contents may be negligently encouraging car-theft by providing thieves with the encouragement of success. From the point of view of the police the by-law is double-edged, because one effect is that they are unlikely to be told of thefts from unlocked cars. This saves paper-work, but prevents them from knowing how prevalent car-thefts are. Nevertheless, there are prohibitions which deserve considera-tion. In Britain, for example, one can obtain a new set of number-plates for a vehicle without being required to produce any evidence of ownership.

ix. The quality of life

Many of the examples in this catalogue of precautions will seem obvious or trivial. A few will sound so drastic as to make the price too high. Few people, it may be said, can be expected to remember or follow all this advice at every relevant juncture. Even if they could, their lives, though less nasty, brutish, and short, would be fussy, costly, and fraught. Yet there are countries, and parts of countries, where that is what life is like for most of the popula-tion. For them the law of the local jungle is more important than the law of the land. This is true not only in the slums of Calcutta or the barrios of Latin America, but also to some extent in the city centres and even the campuses of the USA. It is only in countries which have enjoyed relatively low rates of serious crime for generations that the State is expected to conduct a purely pro-fessional campaign against crime, as if it were fighting a small and far-off war.

x. Are we at war?

'The war against crime' became a fashionable phrase about a quarter of a century ago.[4] Like 'war on want' it was a slogan rather than a genuine declaration. Very few societies behave as if they are really at war with criminals. Even people who are called 'enemies of society' are allowed the protection of inverted commas. We try to take them prisoner, not kill them; and if they are killed in the process we hold an inquiry. Having taken them prisoner we release them before hostilities are over, for if this is a war it has no armistice. We spare, even care for, the prisoners' dependants, instead of bombing or blockading them.

In the skirmishes of this so-called war the police are expected to 'play fair' against people who do not. They must use the minimum of force when faced with violence. They must not fabricate evidence, or obtain true evidence by lies, inducements, threats, or unauthorized searches; yet by convention the defendant can commit perjury without fear of the consequences. These rules, imposed on the police by the courts, are dictated by the negative principle of retribution: that the innocent must not be punished. Better a guilty man go unpunished than an innocent one be punished, thought the Roman jurists. *Twenty* guilty men, said fifteenth-century Fortescue. *Ten*, said seventeenth-century Seymour. *Five*, said his contemporary Hale. The larger the ratio the more imposing the rhetoric: but the point is the same. A mere possibility of innocence outweighs a probability of guilt. So suspects are presumed innocent until courts are sure of their guilt. They have the right to be silent until advised by a lawyer; and he can advise them to remain silent, even in court. There the rules of evidence are in their favour. If convicted they can appeal, whereas in most common-law countries the prosecution cannot. Safeguards built up by earlier generations of lawyers to save the innocent from the gallows now preserve the guilty from probation.

Although offenders themselves feel no obligation to abide by the rules of due process, they make use of them. 'Censoriousness'[5] is one of their tactics. The most powerful propaganda against the agents of criminal justice is that which accuses them not of being ineffective but of bending or breaking the rules: another example of the rule-following cast of mind which was described in Chapter 2. It is a tactic which puts rule-followers at the mercy of rule-breakers, even when both are aware of the tactic. The rules of a society are valued more highly than the well-being of individual members. Chivalry of this sort may be the better policy; but it is not war.

xi. *The war against terrorism*

The contrast between real and metaphorical war is at its most striking when the 'enemies' are terrorists. Unlike the great majority of criminals they make use of the tools as well as the techniques of genuine war. They use firearms and explosives, and select their targets for tactical or strategic reasons (tactical targets are the police, soldiers, and politicians; strategic ones are members of political, ethnic, or national groups). They take prisoners, and use them as hostages. Their political or religious aims justify, in their eyes, the breaking of rules which most criminals honour—for example against killing or maiming children.

Yet few countries' countermeasures are as warlike as they could be. With great reluctance some jurisdictions make membership of certain organizations an imprisonable offence, but allow sympathizers to set up 'political wings' with the same objective. Because terrorism on the modern scale, and with modern weapons and techniques, is a recent development most jurisdictions are still trying to deal with it under the time-honoured rules of the criminal law. Even where special courts without juries are used, as in Northern Ireland, they must observe the ordinary rules of evidence, and be satisfied of guilt beyond reasonable doubt. The possibility of innocence still outweighs the probability of guilt. Terrorists are sometimes shot in hot blood, but seldom executed in cold blood. One result is that hostages are taken by their comrades in the hope of bargaining for their freedom; but the agents of the law do not adopt the same tactic. Captured terrorists are sentenced like other offenders, and often released before hostilities have ceased (a benefit which they forget when asking to be treated as prisoners of war). If this is war, it is a one-sided affair.

There have been tentative efforts to make the rules more warlike. Even when dealing with the ordinary crimes of the 1950s some influential judges such as Goddard began to relax the standard of proof required in criminal trials by merely asking juries to be 'satisfied' of guilt. At first the Court of Criminal Appeal seemed to be tolerating this; but the rule proved too crystalline to bend, and eventually in 1979 the Judicial Committee of the Privy Council made it clear that satisfaction was not enough. Nowadays juries are told that they must be 'satisfied so that you are sure'.[6] In 1972 the Criminal Law Revision Committee argued that the suspect's right to silence at all stages was unduly favourable to him, and it recommended a modification of the rule; but lawyers persuaded Parliament to reject this.[7] It is only where crimes by organized networks are concerned—terrorism and drug-trafficking—that the rule-followers have made warlike concessions. Juryless courts in Northern Ireland and special powers to detain suspected terrorists are examples. More recently, the Drug Trafficking Offences Act 1986 has allowed courts to presume that the whole of a convicted drug-dealer's assets are the proceeds of trafficking, and therefore liable to confiscation: the onus of proving otherwise now lies on him. It is a rule which will be applied before long to other highly organized and lucrative commercial offences. Perhaps terrorism and drug-trafficking will turn out to be social phenomena with sufficient impact to break crystalline rules.

xii. Prevention and criminological theories

Enough has been said in this chapter to demonstrate that the preventive approach is independent of most theorizing about explanations of law-breaking or about the right way to deal with law-breakers when they are identified. 'Preventers' are not necessarily sceptical of such theorizing, although they could draw attention to some of its shortcomings, as I have tried to do in earlier chapters. But answers to the question 'Why do people do that sort of thing?' seldom tell us how to make it difficult or unattractive to do it. More relevant is information of the sort which in Chapter 4 I called 'the natural history of offending'. It is useful to preventers to know what sorts of person are usually responsible for what sorts of crime in what sorts of situation. Occasionally it is useful to know something about rule-breaking states of mind; but more remote contributory factors are hardly ever relevant. As for penological theories, it is only incapacitation that is of much interest to the preventer. Some criminals do such harm, and in such determined or compulsive ways, that he can make out a strong case for putting them out of action. His case, however, must take account of, and try to meet, the anti-protectionist arguments which were outlined in Chapter 10. And if his version of prevention includes ways of reducing acquittal rates he must be intellectually equipped to take on the most formidable group of rule-followers, the legal profession.

17

Politics and Criminology

Like most of the social sciences, criminology has its political undertones and overtones. At the most obvious level, some crimes are politically motivated. Terrorism is not the only example; just the most spectacular. People who would not dream of intentionally killing others commit less serious infringements in order to express their opposition to such things as nuclear armaments, abortion, racialism, vivisection; and a few are even prepared to resort to violence for these ends.

At a more interesting level, ideologues read their own objectives into everyday offences of acquisition by the disadvantaged. Disadvantages such as poverty or unemployment are certainly conditions which provide motives for theft, burglary, robbery, and fraud; but the numbers of disadvantaged thieves, burglars, robbers, or fraudsters who commit their offences in states of mind which amount to conscious political self-justification have been greatly exaggerated. 'Property is theft' is not a plea offered by many law-breakers, even in private conversation. They are more likely, as we saw in 6.vi, to argue that their victims can afford it, or are 'asking for it' by their carelessness; but that is scarcely political discourse.

More plausibly, high crime-rates are cited in support of campaigns for the improvement of conditions such as bad housing, low earnings, and substandard education. This is almost always, however, a subsidiary argument: the main ones are humanitarian or egalitarian, and would stand on their own feet without the assumption that these reforms would reduce the volume of law-breaking. In practice it has never been shown that they have an appreciable effect of this kind. At the same time the prevalence of such beliefs amongst social workers, social reformers and left-of-centre politicians is a political fact.

i. Beliefs of the right and left

It is not only left-wing politicians whose beliefs about crime are simplistic. It is worth comparing the beliefs which tend to be associated with the politics of the right and the left. Right-wingers usually hold

1. that most criminal behaviour is attributable to lax child-rearing, irresponsible parental attitudes, and uncensored television. More extreme, but less common nowadays, is the belief that genetic or congenital defects make an important contribution to crime;
2. that the most effective counter-measures are directed at the individual: deterrence, incapacitation, elimination, confiscation of property, stigma; but that the reform of individuals' characters is a visionary aim;
3. that it is both right and expedient that the scope of the criminal law should cover most forms of conduct which are socially or morally undesirable;
4. and that the need to detect and convict as many offenders as possible justifies expedients such as identity documents, finger-printing, majority verdicts, relaxation of strict rules of evidence, and a narrow interpretation of 'reasonable doubt'.

Left-wingers tend to hold

1. that economic and other social pressures are more important causal factors than family influences, and that genetic or congenital defects are of negligible importance;
2. that deterrence is less effective than re-education and rehabilitation; that the aim of incapacitation seldom—if ever—justifies extremely long periods of detention; and that elimination is morally unacceptable;
3. that the scope of the criminal law should be restricted to forms of conduct which are a serious threat to individuals or society and cannot be controlled by less drastic means;
4. and that the need to protect the innocent against the agencies of law enforcement outweighs the desirability of improving the efficiency of the system.

I have not included in this list the belief that the criminal law itself is 'a major cause of crime' (see 5.i), because it is a revival of scholasticism which seems to be confined to a few left-wing academics. Less silly, however, and more popular is the belief that law-*enforcement* is a major cause of *persistent* law-breaking, because it labels as criminals people who might not repeat their crimes, and so drives them into criminal associations and behaviour. The important point is not the weakness of the evidence for this, but the eagerness with which it was taken up by criminologists in the 1960s, and used in the attempt to discredit law-enforcement.

ii. Common ground?

It is much less easy to distinguish left from right when the retributive justification for penalties is the issue. Historically the duty of the State to administer deserved punishment has been asserted by the right; but the recent revival of retribution, under the name of 'just deserts' (see Chapter 11) has found supporters on both sides of the divide. Their reasoning is not the same. Left-wingers tend to see just deserts as a principle which sets desirable limits to the severity of penal measures. It rules out, for example, sentences which detain offenders for periods which greatly exceed the standard term for the offence of which they have been found guilty, although even some anti-protectionists (see 10.iii) concede exceptions in the case of offenders who are seen as very dangerous to others. For right-wingers the principle provides a justification for penalizing an offender when this seems unlikely to achieve any instrumental aim. These two lines of reasoning however are not contradictory. The two armies can unite under a single banner, so long as they are not cross-examined about the meaning of 'desert' (see 11.iii).

Another area of considerable agreement is prevention, in the sense in which the term is used in Chapter 16. Strategies for making crimes more difficult to commit, or more likely to lead to the identification of the offender or his ill-gotten gains, seem acceptable to almost every shade of political opinion. It is only subsidiary issues that provoke argument. Can the State afford to subsidize precautions by those who cannot meet the cost themselves? Should people be penalized for failing to take easy precautions, such as locking their cars? At what point does healthy neighbourhood vigilance become unhealthy vigilantism? These are peripheral questions.

iii. Politicians and voters

A distinction must be drawn, however, between active and passive politics: between politicians and the people who merely vote for them. Although 'law and order' has been a banner of the right and a target of the left, it is really a screen which hides an important gap between the concerns of politicians and voters. Order is what matters to politicians. Freedom from crime is what voters value. When politicians are in power, collective disorder or disobedience is a direct threat. When they are in opposition, they are slightly ambivalent about such happenings. Extremists encourage them; moderates deplore them, but make political capital out of them. The ordinary voter, who can usually steer clear of demonstrations, pickets, and riots, is more anxious about the possibility of being robbed, burgled, raped, or defrauded by some apolitical criminal.

So politicians of both right and left must talk as if their societies were really at war with criminals. Moreover their talk must be optimistic. They must be seen to have plans, whatever the lessons of history or experimentation. A stock response, for example, to public alarm about the prevalence of some type of crime is legislation to increase the maximum penalty. In practice this seldom induces sentencers to raise the tariff. The armchair thoughts of politicians are apt to override the experience of professionals. A recent Home Secretary decided to intensify the unpleasantness of detention centres for young males by devoting more of their time to hard exercise and military drill. The decision misfired because—as professionals could have told him, and researchers could have confirmed—young males prefer such activities to scrubbing floors and digging vegetable gardens. It was the staff who found the changes uncongenial. More successful, in a political sense, has been the promotion of probation. The use of it has been encouraged by governments of both colours, in the face of strong evidence that it succeeds only when used very

selectively. The unselective way in which courts are encouraged
to use it has only one advantage. As a prelude to the offender's
next conviction, it is cheaper than custody. Yet the Home
Office's handbook for sentencers presents probation as a
success.[1]

iv. *The politics of incarceration*

The 'politics of incarceration' are interesting, too. Because most
other countries in Western Europe have fewer males in custody
per 100,000 of their population than does Britain, it is assumed
that our prison population should be smaller. The assumption
suits both humanitarians and economists, although both ought to
be asking how the optimum level should be determined. In what
sort of scales should cost be weighed against harm and fear? It
being taken for granted, however, that the optimum level should
be lower, there are two approaches, not inconsistent but favoured
by different schools of thought. One is the avoidance of custodial
sentences for a larger percentage of offenders. This is to be
achieved partly by 'educating' sentencers, although 'propaganda'
would be a more honest term, since education needs facts. Some
proposals involve decriminalizing certain types of behaviour
altogether, forgetting that the aim is merely to avoid custody. The
other approach is the shortening rather than the avoidance of
custodial sentences. The main obstacle has been the doctrine that
the executive must not interfere directly with the discretion which
the statutes confer on judges and magistrates so far as sentence-
lengths are concerned: only Parliament can do this, and only by
legislating maxima. The obstacle has been quietly side-stepped
since 1967 by the device of parole, which makes it possible to
release before his due date any prisoner serving a sentence of ten
and a half months or more. Effectively, control over the time
which these prisoners spend inside has now passed to the Parole
Board and the Home Secretary. Most voters do not realize that
nowadays the judge's sentence merely determines how long the
prisoner *can* be detained, not how long he *will* be.[2] To emphasize
this is not to condemn parole, nor to argue that judges should
have complete control over periods of detention. The point is the
success of a political by-pass.

v. The new penology

Political thinking has also influenced criminological research. In both the UK and the USA the study of law-breakers has been largely replaced by the study of law-enforcers. Police, juries, judges, magistrates, and prison staff have been the main subjects of attention (probation officers have received much less). Researchers have sought, and inevitably found, evidence of rule-breaking and improper use of discretionary power. Class bias, sexism, and racialism have been unearthed. The effect has been salutary. Law-enforcers are more responsive to exposure than law-breakers. Moreover, they are remarkably willing to submit to investigation, which makes this kind of research less difficult and more likely to yield results than the study of elusive and reticent criminals who keep no records of their decisions. It would be unfair, however, to ascribe this switch of attention entirely to the fact that law-enforcers are easier game. An important motive has been liberals' suspicion of the agencies of the State, and in particular the agencies of 'law and order'. Civil liberty is a powerful watch-word. But one result has been that criminologists and penologists who study the natural history of offending or the behaviour of offenders in prison or under supervision are now outnumbered by those who concentrate on law-enforcers. We need a new occupational term for this kind of penology.

vi. Feminist criminology

Of all the biases of which law-enforcers are suspected, sexism is currently the most topical. The politics of feminism are of interest to an even larger constituency than the politics of racialism. The very fact that females, whether young or adult, make such a small contribution to official and unofficial statistics of offending is the most striking thing in criminology. Attempts have been made to tone it down, by arguing either that females are more skilled in concealment or—more plausibly—that their deviant behaviour more often breaches social norms than criminal codes. The main topics of feminist criminology, however, have been the invisible victimization of women and the bias with which women offenders are handled by police, courts, social workers, and custodial staff. The forms of invisible victimization which have received most ention are rape and domestic violence, both of which are probably under-recorded because of the scepticism with which police are believed to treat such incidents (see 15.i). The reputation of feminist criminology has suffered from the extreme statements of a few pioneers: for example that 'most men in the USA are potential rapists . . . The rapist is the man next door'.[3] By the same token the infanticide is the mother next door. But it would be unfair to imply that such reasoning is typical.

Sexist bias in law-enforcement, too, may be real or illusory. Police and courts were once believed to be chivalrously lenient towards women, until researchers showed that women's crimes, though bearing the same legal labels as men's, were usually less serious, and that their criminal records were more reassuring. Nowadays the pendulum has swung, and courts are suspected of using custodial measures for women when they would not apply them to a man in similar circumstances. The evidence offered is usually the fact that higher percentages of women prisoners are first offenders. But since in any sound sample of offenders a larger fraction of the men will have previous convictions, this is only what one would expect if courts were sentencing men and women without any sexist bias. It is as if doctors were accused of sexism because fewer women in hospital have previous histories of traffic accidents. The real biases are too subtle to show up in the judicial statistics.

vii. *Ignoring the signposts*

This chapter is not meant to do justice to the good intentions of politicians, feminists, or criminologists. What it should have demonstrated is that ideological reasoning is not confined to politicians; and that where criminology and penology are concerned it leads up false trails, sheep-tracks, and abandoned paths. The warning signposts erected by less ideological historians and social scientists are overlooked, brushed aside, or even torn down. Ideologies deserve most of the blame: but the signposts are not always well designed. Many are half-buried in journals, or phrased with such precision and caution that they cannot compete with rhetoric. Equally important is the fact that nearly all of them are negative warnings. It is extremely rare to find one that says

'This is the way'; and when one does it is usually the work of a charlatan. As this book has shown, the findings of criminology are not entirely negative; but they point to no royal road: only to footholds.

Notes

Chapter 1: Subjects and Objects

1. Prosecution by police forces, the usual procedure for most indictable and non-indictable offences in England, was abandoned in 1986 with the creation of a nation-wide prosecution service, although prosecutions are still conducted by other agencies such as the Inland Revenue or local authorities responsible for the enforcement of special statutes or by-laws.
2. E. M. Lemert, *Social Pathology*, New York, McGraw-Hill, 1951.
3. Erving Goffman appreciated this, and criticized the widespread assumption that 'deviance' was a single definable field for study; but he was ignored by 'deviologists'. See his *Stigma: Notes on the Management of Spoiled Identity*, Englewood Cliffs, Prentice-Hall, 1963.

Chapter 2: Laws and Rules

1. See H. Garfinkel, *Studies in Ethnomethodology*, Englewood Cliffs, Prentice-Hall, 1967; R. Harré and P. F. Secord, *The Explanation of Social Behaviour*, Oxford, Blackwell, 1972; P. Collet (ed.), *Social Rules and Social Behaviour*, Oxford, Blackwell, 1977; S. Roberts, *Order and Dispute: an Introduction to Legal Anthropology*, Harmondsworth, Penguin, 1979.
2. It is tempting, but not sufficiently accurate, to say that there is a similar exemption for the 'insane'. In fact they are exempt only if, at the time when they infringed a criminal prohibition, their mental state was such as to excuse them. But that is a rule which applies to anyone, insane or not, who infringes the criminal law (see 2.vi.d).
3. They cannot of course control *informal* reactions to someone who is believed to have broken a law.
4. But is often accepted as a reason for mitigating the penalty. Norway is unusual in allowing ignorance of law to be offered as a defence to many kinds of charge.
5. This applies also to some codes of rules: for example to the disciplinary codes of the armed services and the prison service.

Chapter 3: Fictions and Figures

1. E. H. Sutherland, *Professional Thief*, University of Chicago Press, 1937; T. Parker, *The Courage of his Convictions*, London, Hutchinson, 1962; *Five Women*, London, Hutchinson, 1965.
2. D. Curtis, *From Dartmoor to Cambridge*, London, Hodder and Stoughton, 1973; J. Boyle, *A Sense of Freedom*, London, Pan, 1977.
3. G. Mars, *Cheats at Work*, London, Allen and Unwin, 1982; J. Ditton, *Part-Time Crime*, London, Macmillan, 1977; M. Lasswell, *Wellington Road*, Harmondsworth, Penguin, 1969; L. Taylor, *In the Underworld*, Oxford, Blackwell, 1984.
4. See J. D. J. Havard, *The Detection of Secret Homicide*, London, Macmillan, 1960.
5. But this information is not given for attempted murder.
6. Or prosecutors' files; but most of their information comes from the police.
7. In some cases, of course, the offender is also known to the police as a result of indictable offences, in which case their files are likely—but not certain—to mention his income-tax evasions, social security frauds, and other non-indictable misdoings.
8. For example P. H. Ennis, *Criminal Victimisation in the United States*, Washington, U.S. Government Printing Office, 1967.
9. 'Populations' in the technical sense: that is, defined categories of people, such as 'males and females over the age of 18'. Interviews with very young children would have been very difficult to manage, although when achieved they sometimes reveal physical or sexual abuse which would otherwise escape notice.
10. It is important to draw a sharp distinction between *criminal* and *judicial* statistics so far as accuracy is concerned. The latter deal with proceedings in court (or cautions by the police: see 7.ii) and do not conceal a 'dark figure' of unreported cases. They have their own shortcomings: they show, for example, only the numbers of offenders prosecuted and found guilty without distinguishing those who pleaded 'guilty' from those who pleaded 'not guilty'. They do not distinguish offenders with relevant previous convictions (or cautions) from those without them: a very serious defect. They show only the most severe sentence passed, and omit any other sentence for other offences of which the offender may have been convicted in the course of the same 'appearance'. They are thus less informative than they could be, but not to any important extent inaccurate.

Chapter 4: Natural History

1. Although there do seem to be identifiable 'types' of especially inept drivers: see for example S. Quenault, *Driver Behaviour: Safe and Unsafe Drivers*, RRL Report LR70, Transport and Road Research Laboratory, Crowthorne, 1967.

2. That is, obtaining goods on credit, for resale, without the intention of paying the suppliers (apart, perhaps, from one or two initial payments in order to establish credit-worthiness).

3. The 'standard list' includes all indictable offences and a few others which resemble such offences, but not the sort of traffic offence which can be tried only by magistrates, or those involving prostitution or drunkenness, or a host of minor regulatory offences.

4. For statistics about this and later cohorts, see Home Office Statistical Bulletin 7/85 (*Criminal Careers of Those Born in 1953, 1958 and 1963*).

5. In England an offence is counted as 'cleared up' when the police identify at least one of the offenders involved, even if he is not successfully prosecuted. Official clear-up rates for common offences are nowadays suspect. Detectives can inflate them to their credit by inducing offenders who are serving sentences to admit to burglaries, thefts, and so forth which they may or may not have committed: prosecution for them is very unlikely. Even at the sentencing stage, offenders can be persuaded to ask for numbers of unprosecuted offences to be 'taken into consideration'. The effect on the severity of the sentence is slight, and they are thereafter immune from prosecution for those offences. Adding a few offences which they have not committed makes no difference.

6. Suppose, for example, that the probability of 'getting away with' a burglary is 0.6. For two burglaries it is $0.6 \times 0.6 = 0.36$; for three it is $0.6^3 = 0.216$; and so on. Even if the probability for each burglary varies, the probability must decrease with the length of the series, although increasing experience no doubt increases the likelihood of getting away with each of the later burglaries in the series.

7. The Department of Health and Social Security seldom prosecutes frauds involving small amounts.

8. For a thorough study of juvenile networks, see J. Sarnecki, *Delinquent Networks*, Stockholm, National Council for Crime Prevention, Sweden, 1986.

Chapter 5: Behaviour and Misbehaviour

1. See S. Cohen, 'The Failures of Criminology', in *The Listener*, 6 November 1973, 622 ff.; I. Taylor, P. Walton, and J. Young, *The*

New Criminology, London, Routledge and Kegan Paul, 1973. But the fallacy was originally revived by T. Sarbin and J. E. Miller, 'Demonism Revisited', in *Issues in Criminology*, Berkeley, 1970.

2. See D. J. West and D. P. Farrington, *Who Becomes Delinquent?*, London, Heinemann, 1973.

3. Not 89 per cent, as the Gluecks carelessly claimed. For an explanation of their mistake, see West and Farrington, *Who Becomes Delinquent?*.

4. See S. A. Mednick and K. O. Christiansen (edd.), *Biosocial Bases of Criminal Behaviour*, New York, Gardner, 1977.

5. Social scientists like to cite suicide as an example of human action. The tendency is strongly associated with having read Durkheim.

6. Stoufer's term for the sense of deprivation felt by a person or group when they believe another person or group to be more affluent or privileged. It can thus be felt by members of affluent societies in which wealth is unevenly distributed. Some people call it 'envy'.

7. See N. Walker, *Behaviour and Misbehaviour*, Oxford, Blackwell, 1977.

8. He did not make the mistake of saying 'always'. Some historians are interested only in developments for which they can formulate probability explanations, for example of an economic kind.

Chapter 6: Rule-Breaking and Rationality

1. See for example G. Sykes and D. Matza, 'Techniques of Neutralization', *American Sociological Review*, 22 (1957), 664 ff.; M. Phillipson, *Sociological Aspects of Crime and Delinquency*, London, Routledge and Kegan Paul, 1971; H. Toch, *Violent Men: an Inquiry into the Psychology of Violence*, Harmondsworth, Penguin, 1972; H. Garfinkel, *Studies in Ethnomethodology*, Englewood Cliffs, Prentice-Hall, 1967.

2. Some lawyers, following Aristotle, say that it is because everyone ought to make sure, before engaging in any activity, that he knows the relevant law: but this is a counsel of perfection indeed.

3. They were eventually convicted of murder, but their death sentences were commuted to six months' imprisonment: a clear indication that they were regarded as justified in disapplying the rule.

4. G. Sykes and D. Matza, 'Techniques of Neutralization', *American Sociological Review*, 22 (1957), 664 ff.

5. R. Dworkin, *Taking Rights Seriously*, London, Duckworth, 1977.

6. In *John Bull's Other Island*.

7. But see (in 6.xiv) the ridiculous generalization which Glover based on this, in *The Roots of Crime: Selected Papers on Psycho-Analysis*,

New York, International Universities Press, 1964. Freud needed protection from his friends.

8. See E. H. Sutherland, *Principles of Criminology*, Philadelphia, Lippincott, 1947; D. Matza, *Delinquency and Drift*, New York, London, John Wiley, 1964; M. Wolfgang and F. Ferracuti, *The Sub-Culture of Violence: towards an Integrated Theory in Criminology*, London, Tavistock, 1967; E. M. Lemert, *Human Deviance, Social Problems and Social Control*, Englewood Cliffs, Prentice-Hall, 1969; T. R. Fyvel, *Social Deviance: Social Policy, Action and Research*, London, Tavistock, 1961.

9. See J. Dollard and N. Miller *et al.*, *Frustration and Aggression*, New Haven, Yale University Press, 1939.

10. See D. Cressey, *Other Peoples' Money*, Glencoe, Free Press, 1953.

11. See É. Durkheim, *The Rules of Sociological Method* (1895), 1950 translation, Glencoe, Free Press.

Chapter 7: Sentencing and Not Sentencing

1. See, for instance, S. and E. T. Glueck, *Predicting Delinquency and Crime*, New York, Harper, 1950.

2. See E. Powers and H. Witmer, *An Experiment in the Prevention of Delinquency: the Cambridge-Somerville Youth Study*, Columbia University Press, 1951.

3. But, confusingly, this term is used, especially in the USA, to include measures ordered by criminal courts as substitutes for incarceration.

4. His chances seem lower under the 'inquisitorial' systems of trial in Continental Europe.

5. Note that a civil suit is decided 'on a balance of probabilities', yet may result in the award of damages which are far more severe than the fine of a criminal court would be.

6. A defence which was so common in the case of car-borrowing that it was countered by creating the offence of 'taking for one's own use without the owner's consent'. Yet book-borrowing without a librarian's consent is not similarly countered.

7. The order is usually, but not always, a 'sentence'. Probation orders, hospital orders (for the mentally disordered), and recommendations for deportation, compensation, or restriction orders are not sentences.

8. Another moral argument is that mistaken executions can never be put right if the mistake is discovered. But this seems to imply that if there is no mistake the penalty is justified.

9. An interesting exception is G. Newman, *Just and Painful: a Case for the Corporal Punishment of Criminals*, London, Macmillan, 1983,

which argues that flogging and painful electric shocks are preferable to incarceration.

10. Deportation may have more drastic and lasting consequences for some offenders, but is limited to non-citizens. Commitment for an indefinite period to a mental hospital is feared by most offenders more than a custodial sentence; but only a minority are eligible.

11. Although this recommendation does not bind the executive, and is now and again overridden by Home Secretaries.

12. Or, very occasionally, to protect him against retaliation.

13. Heavy drinkers, however, may become depressed on being deprived of the alcohol which they have been using as an anti-depressant.

14. See R. J. Sapsford, *Life Sentence Prisoners: Reaction, Response and Change*, Milton Keynes, Open University Press, 1983; J. Coker, letter in *British Journal of Criminology*, 23: 2 (1983), 307 ff. For a critical review of the research on unwanted side-effects, see N. Walker, 'The Unwanted Effects of Long-Term Imprisonment' in *Problems of Long-Term Imprisonment*, A. E. Bottoms and R. Light (edd.), London, Gower, 1987.

15. Scottish courts provide every accused person who might conceivably be fined with a form on which he is invited, but not obliged, to declare his means. English magistrates' courts have been advised to follow suit, but many have exercised their freedom to disregard advice.

16. In petty cases he can be detained in the court-house or in police cells for very short periods. Courts which use this power—by no means all do—have usually despaired of extracting any more payments. Short-term visitors from abroad are sometimes dealt with in this way if they have spent all the money they have with them.

17. A third criticism of the system is that many courts are inefficient at keeping track of unpaid fines, so that collection is months in arrears.

18. Not the victims: that is 'reparation': see 15.iv.

19. The supervision of offenders under 14 is the responsibility of local authorities' social work departments.

20. See A. E. Bottoms and W. McWilliams, 'Social Enquiry Reports Twenty-Five Years after the Streatfeild Report', in *Barbara Wootton: Essays in her Honour*, P. Bean and D. Whynes (edd.), London, Tavistock, 1986.

21. A suspended sentence can be combined with supervision, as it usually is in France, for example. In France fines too can be suspended. Partial suspension—a recent and rather hasty innovation—complicates unnecessarily a system which already includes remission and parole.

Chapter 8: Sentences and Justifications

1. It is better to talk of 'penalizing' than of 'punishing', since 'punishment' is so often taken as implying a retributive aim.

2. Sometimes called 'rehabilitation', although it is better to reserve this term for efforts to make it *easier* for the offender to live a law-abiding life, for example by providing him with a job. This needs to be distinguished from efforts to improve his attitude to law-breaking. But 'reform' is nowadays a somewhat discredited term, so that 'rehabilitation' is used with almost deliberate ambiguity.

3. See G. J. O. Phillpotts and L. B. Lancucki, *Previous Convictions, Sentence and Reconviction*, London, HMSO, 1979, and the further analysis by N. Walker, D. Farrington, and G. Tucker, 'Reconvictions of Adult Males after Different Sentences', in *British Journal of Criminology*, 21: 4 (1981), 357 ff.

4. See R. Martinson, 'What Works?', in *Public Interest*, Spring 1974, 22 ff. and 'New Findings, New Views: a Note of Caution Regarding Sentencing Reform', in *Hofstra Law Review*, 7: 2 (1979), 243 ff. His use of statistics suggests that he had not grasped all the methodological problems.

5. See C. Eichmann, *The Impact of the Gideon Decision upon Crime and Sentencing in Florida*, Florida Department of Corrections, 1966; D. Jaman *et al.*, 'Parole Outcome as a Function of Time Served', in *British Journal of Criminology*, 12: 1 (1972), 5 ff.

6. *Prison Statistics, England and Wales*, London, HMSO.

Chapter 9: Deterrence and Education

1. The most striking comparisons were those in the *Report of the Royal Commission on Capital Punishment*, E. Gowers (chairman), Cmd. 8932, London, HMSO, 1954. Ehrlich's 1975 article, purporting to show that each execution in the USA saved the nation about eight homicides (plus or minus twelve!) has been the subject of telling criticisms, summarized by Hann (1977): see I. Ehrlich, 'The Deterrent Effect of Capital Punishment: a Question of Life or Death', in *American Economic Review*, 65 (1975), 397 ff.; and R. G. Hann, *Deterrence and the Death Penalty: a Critical Review of the Research of Isaac Ehrlich*, Ottawa, Research Division of the Solicitor General of Canada, 1977.

2. As when would-be shop-lifters get children under the age of criminal liability to do their stealing.

3. For a review of the effects of 'Scandinavian-type' legislation in various jurisdictions, see L. Ross, *Deterring the Drinking Driver:*

Legal Policy and Social Control, Lexington, Lexington Books, 1982.

4. See R. D. Schwartz and S. Orleans, 'On Legal Sanctions', in *University of Chicago Law Review*, 34 (1967), 274 ff.

5. See D. Lewis, 'The General Deterrent Effect of Longer Sentences', in *British Journal of Criminology*, 26: 1 (1986), 47 ff.

6. See J. Andenaes, *Punishment and Deterrence*, Ann Arbor, University of Michigan Press, 1974. Although Ross (see n. 3) is sceptical, it seems unlikely that the compliance is due to estimates of the (not very high) probability of being detected.

7. See N. Walker and C. Marsh, 'Do Sentences Affect Public Disapproval?', in *British Journal of Criminology*, 24: 1 (1984), 27 ff.

8. See R. Baxter and C. Nuttall, 'Severe Sentences: No Deterrent to Crime?', in *New Society*, 31 (1975), 11 ff.

9. The most thorough review is by D. Beyleveld in *A Bibliography on General Deterrence Research*, Westmead, Saxon House, 1980.

10. Examples are campaigns to discourage drunken driving at Christmas time.

11. It is necessary to mention, if not to take very seriously, the claim that deterrents are used only to maintain the political status quo. Apart from the naïve implication that anything is better than the status quo, it is obviously untrue that political innovators never use deterrents. New regimes often enforce changes by very harsh penalties. Nor are deterrents used only by those in power: terrorists, by definition, use them.

12. An argument credited to Kant, although exactly what he meant is the subject of discussion which is hardly relevant here: see T. Honderich, *Punishment: the Supposed Justifications*, London, Hutchinson, 1969.

13. Deterrents are not the only penalties which can be criticized on this ground: precautionary detention (see Chapter 10) is open to the same objection.

14. Or, more precisely, what is believed to be the usual sentence.

15. For a short history of this idea, see N. Walker, 'The Ultimate Justification', in *Crime, Proof and Punishment: Essays in Memory of Sir Rupert Cross*, C. Tapper (ed.), London, Butterworths, 1981.

16. See, for example, Sir Walter Moberly, *The Ethics of Punishment*, London, Faber and Faber, 1968; J. Feinberg, *Doing and Deserving*, Princeton University Press, 1970.

17. It is not really an aspect of retribution, because it is not essential to it that the sentence should actually be carried out. A suspended sentence is an example.

18. See N. Walker and C. Marsh, 'Do Sentences Affect Public

Disapproval?', in *British Journal of Criminology*, 24: 1 (1984), 27 ff. The offences had to be of only moderate seriousness because pilot experiments had shown that for more serious crimes respondents' levels of disapproval were so high that no effect could be detected, at least by the experimental method used.

19. Sir Walter Moberly in *The Ethics of Punishment* also believed that sentences can have a 'Sargeant effect' on the sentencer and on the person sentenced, reinforcing the former's disapproval and impressing the latter with society's disapproval. Allison Morris *et al.*, *Justice for Children*, London, Macmillan, 1980, say that it has this effect on juvenile offenders. Certainly one can at least be sure that both the sentencer and the sentenced know what sentence has been passed (although some juveniles are confused about it). So far as the offender is concerned it is possible that the sentence has this desirable effect, always provided that he accepts it as a just sentence. He may of course become less acceptant as time 'inside' wears on, or in the course of paying instalments of a heavy fine. As for the possibility that sentencers reinforce their own or each other's disapproval of the offence, it is arguable that by doing so they insulate themselves against the views of people who disapprove less (or more, as in the case of recent English sentences for rape).

20. See H. Gross, *A Theory of Criminal Justice*, London, Oxford University Press, 1979, pp. 400–1. But it is odd to assert that the threats of the criminal law 'are not laid down to deter' when the history of penal legislation clearly says that they were.

21. A symbolic theory is one which finds the justification for the sentence in the message conveyed by it rather than its actual or supposed consequences for the offender or potential imitators.

Chapter 10: Incapacitation and Dangerousness

1. For a fuller list, see Appendix F of N. Walker, *Sentencing: Theory, Law and Practice*, London, Butterworths, 1985.
2. See 8.ii.
3. See J. Petersilia *et al.*, *Granting Felons Probation: Public Risks*, Santa Monica, Rand, 1985.
4. Leeds, where the social services department and the probation department set up a monitoring scheme for teenagers in 1982, according to their unpublished interim report (1984).
5. See N. Walker, 'Unscientific, Unwise, Unprofitable or Unjust?', in *British Journal of Criminology*, 22: 3 (1982), 276 ff.
6. See J. Floud and W. Young, *Dangerousness and Criminal Justice*, London, Heinemann, 1981.

7. See P. W. Greenwood and A. Abrahamse, *Selective Incapacitation*, Santa Monica, Rand, 1982. Their report, however, does not make it clear by how much the normal periods of detention would have to be increased or reduced.

8. Manslaughter, attempted murder, rape, buggery of a person, sexual intercourse or incest with a girl under 13, aggravated burglary, robbery or assault with intent to rob, criminal damage with intent to endanger life, and wounding with intent to do grievous bodily harm. For murder life is mandatory.

9. But the policies of recent Home Secretaries have declared an explicit semi-official minimum of twenty years for some categories of offence, for retributive or deterrent reasons. Indeterminate detention in mental hospitals, though also subject to executive control, is not subject to explicit minima of this kind.

10. Examples of exceptions are cases in which psychiatrists can say that a mental illness can be successfully treated within a foreseeably short period; or in which the only victim likely to be attacked is dead or beyond the offender's reach.

Chapter 11: Desert and Ritual

1. It is also necessary to mention a quibble beloved of English moral philosophers. If a penalty is inflicted on someone who is *wrongly believed* to have transgressed, is it 'punishment'? The sensible answer seems to be that if the belief in his guilt is sincere, and if the penalty was inflicted for retributive reasons, it *is* punishment, but of the kind which we call 'mistaken punishment'.

2. See his *Punishment and Responsibility*, London, Oxford University Press, 1968.

3. J. G. Cottingham rests this claim on a short passage in which Kant talks of *Blutschuld* (blood-guilt): see his article 'Varieties of Retribution' in *Philosophical Quarterly*, 29 (1979), 23 ff. This interpretation is a heavy burden for a single word.

4. By T. Honderich, *Punishment: the Supposed Justifications*, London, Hutchinson, 1969.

5. For my original version of this suggestion, see *Punishment, Danger and Stigma*, Oxford, Blackwell, 1980.

6. I have more to say about this in *Sentencing: Theory, Law and Practice*, London, Butterworths, 1985.

7. Bentham, who listed more than thirty factors affecting an offender's 'sensibility' to punishment, included 'nobility'; and even today some sentencers reason that a person's social standing may be

so adversely affected by the stigma of conviction that the official penalty can be lightened.

8. See, for example, A. R. N. Cross, *The English Sentencing System*, London, Butterworths, 1971.

9. See his *Punishment and Responsibility*, London, Oxford University Press, 1968.

10. The Law Society's First Memorandum to the Royal Commission on the Penal System (1967), which talked of the 'D(isapprobation) Factor' as a non-retributive non-instrumental justification of punishment is clearly of this sort, but without being explicitly worked out. The Canadian Law Reform Commission's Report *Our Criminal Law* also suggests this symbolic justification, but wastes no space on it.

Chapter 12: Juveniles and Justice

1. There is a similar over-representation of teenagers amongst women who are detected in offences.

2. The technical term introduced by Wolfgang in his study of Philadelphians' criminal careers. 'Desistance' can of course be real or illusory: the offender may simply have learned how to avoid detection. Only self-reporting studies can tell the difference, and then not always.

3. Interestingly, before and for some time after the Norman Conquest the age was quite high: 14, at least for felonies. In the Middle Ages it was lowered to 7 under the influence of the Church (since 7 was the age at which a child could confess to sin). In 1932 it was raised to 8 in Britain; and in 1963 to 10 in England. Scotland kept the age at 8, but uses a non-criminal system of 'children's hearings' to deal with juveniles under 16, except in cases of murder and other very serious crimes.

4. Where the age was originally based on the Roman age of puberty (14), but has since been raised to 15 or even higher. This does not, however, prevent under-age delinquents from being subjected to compulsory removal from home, or other measures, under 'welfare' legislation.

5. Lord Goddard did add that the parents should have been prosecuted for larceny as bailees or larceny by finding. He clearly felt that *they* should not be regarded as guiltless. His solution was not without its own fictitious elements. The parents had not, for example, 'found' the tricycle: their son had brought it home. But Goddard cannot be blamed for trying to make the law do justice. Nor can the draftsmen of the 1932 Act be blamed for their 'conclusive presumption': they were merely putting the common law into statute.

6. In Scotland, 16. The 'care' may last for a year or so after that age, but must have begun before it.

7. A practice which was eventually extended to adults' courts.

8. The percentages vary from one area to another, but efforts are being made to reduce the variation.

9. Between his fourteenth and seventeenth birthdays a juvenile is called a 'young person' in the statutes; before 14 he is a 'child'. Between his seventeenth and twenty-first birthdays he is a 'young adult'.

10. He need not be shown to have known it was criminal if he can be shown to have known it was morally wrong. Interestingly, the rule for the insanity defence is different: the defendant is excusable only if his 'disease of the mind' made him fail to realize that his act was criminal, not if it made him think it was morally permissible.

11. But not after he reaches the age of 21, if the finding occurred before he was 14.

12. The technical term for choosing the measure which seems best suited to the individual's personality and situation, as distinct from the measure usually considered appropriate for the offence. Obviously the extent to which courts can 'individualize' is limited by the choices allowed by statute. They can only hope that the staff who carry out the measure will be more flexible.

13. See A. Morris *et al.*, *Justice for Children*, London, Macmillan, 1980. Yet they also advocate an extensive use of diversion from prosecution, provided that the criteria for non-prosecution are fair and consistently applied. Their point is that there should be *some* official reaction to juveniles' offences, even if this is only a chat with a policeman.

14. Morris and Giller interviewed a small sample of juveniles and parents about their impressions of court proceedings, but without concentrating on the educational aim. Parker *et al.* interviewed somewhat larger samples, from areas of benches with quite different sentencing policies, but were more concerned with other aspects, such as arrest, pre-trial detention, and the intelligibility of the proceedings.

Chapter 13: Anonymity and Stigma

1. The committee which recommended this complicated system reasoned hypocritically. 'Clearly,' they said, 'the more serious the offence the longer it will be before one can be reasonably sure that the offender has reformed' (they assumed that the severity of the sentence would reflect the seriousness of the offence). This was contrary to the known facts: it is the petty offender who is the most

repetitive. They added, however, that to treat all offenders alike as regards the rehabilitation period would be 'too radical to command general support', thus revealing their real reasoning. See Lord Gardiner (chairman), *Living it Down: the Problem of Old Convictions*, London, Stevens, 1970. For a fuller description of the provisions of the Rehabilitation of Offenders Act 1974, see N. Walker, *Sentencing: Theory, Law and Practice*, London, Butterworths, 1985.

2. In Britain pardons can be granted, but are reserved for cases in which the conviction turns out to have been unjust, and are not used simply to 'rehabilitate' the justly convicted.

3. For some evidence, and a good review of other evidence, see D. P. Farrington's two articles 'The Effects of Public Labelling', in *British Journal of Criminology*, 17: 2 (1977), 112 ff.; and (with S. G. Osborn and D. J. West) 'The Persistence of Labelling Effects', in *British Journal of Criminology*, 18: 3 (1978), 277 ff. See also C. Tittle, 'Labelling and Crime: an Evaluation', in *The Labelling of Deviance*, W. Gove (ed.), London, Sage, 1980.

4. See also J. L. Freedman and A. L. Doob, *Deviancy: the Psychology of being Different*, New York, Academic Press, 1968. Curiously, although this describes one of the few good experiments which provide some support for labelling claims, it is hardly ever cited by labelling theorists.

5. See H. D. Willcock and J. Stokes, *Deterrents to Crime amongst Youths aged 15 to 21*, London, Government Social Survey (not on sale).

Chapter 14: Criminalizing and Decriminalizing

1. See C. B. Beccaria, *Dei Delitti e delle Pene* (1764): first English translation, London, Almon, 1767.

2. But nowadays in England bigamy is prosecuted only in cases in which one of the partners has deceived the other, and done so for financial gain or seduction.

3. See John Stuart Mill, *On Liberty*, London, Parker, 1859 (in John Stuart Mill, *Three Essays*, Oxford University Press paperback edition, 1975), Ch. I, para. 9.

4. H. L. A. Hart, *The Morality of the Criminal Law: Two Essays*, London, Oxford University Press, 1965.

5. John Stuart Mill, *On Liberty*, Ch. IV, para. 11.

6. C. de S. Montesquieu, *L'Esprit des Lois* (1748): first English translation, London, Nourse and Vaillant, 1750.

7. James Fitzjames Stephen, *Liberty, Equality, Fraternity*, London,

Smith, Elder, 1873, Ch. IV, para. 55. (The title was sarcastic.)

8. See Mr Adair's Minority Report appended to Sir John F. Wolfenden, *Report of the Committee on Homosexual Offences and Prostitution*, Cmd. 247, London, HMSO, 1955. Mr Adair represented Scotland, where the Committee's recommendations for liberalizing the law as regards homosexual acts were not implemented until long after they had been adopted in England.

9. Hansard, Commons, 23 April 1968.

10. See L. Berkowitz and N. Walker, 'Laws and Moral Judgements', in *Sociometry*, 30: 4 (1967), 410 ff.

11. See N. Walker and C. Marsh, 'Do Sentences Affect Public Disapproval?', in *British Journal of Criminology*, 24: 1 (1984), 27 ff. Some of the subjects were told that when not wearing a seat-belt became illegal it would be punishable with a fine, some were told that it would be punishable with imprisonment, but some were given no information about the penalty; and the information about the penalty seemed to make no difference. All three groups were more disapproving when not wearing a seat-belt became an offence.

12. See P. Devlin, *The Enforcement of Morals*, London, Oxford University Press, 1959, p. 5.

13. The problem becomes more acute, however, when an activity is prohibited only because of its political objectives: as when a book is banned or a demonstration prohibited because of the message which it is intended to convey. The 'right to free speech' has been powerfully asserted in Britain and the USA, although when claimed by racists or paedophiles it worries even liberals.

Chapter 15: Victims and Victimology

1. Even young children may do this, according to L. Burton, *Vulnerable Children*, London, Routledge and Kegan Paul, 1968.

2. As has been pointed out by R. A. Silverman, 'Victim Precipitation: an Examination of the Concept', in *Victimology: a New Focus*, I. Drapkin and E. Viano (edd.), Lexington, Heath, 1974.

3. Unfortunately this does not completely dispose of the problem where rape is concerned. The defendant can plead that he believed that the woman was consenting, and the belief does not have to be a 'reasonable' one. Of course the grounds which he alleges for his belief may be so ridiculous that the jury are entitled to *dis*believe his assertion about his belief. But if they accept his plea as true then however ridiculous his grounds they must acquit him. Some men genuinely believe that hitch-hiking is a sign of willingness.

4. See C. Jones and E. Aronson, 'Attribution of Fault to a Rape Victim

as a Function of Respectability of the Rape Victim', in *Journal of Personal and Social Psychology*, 26 (1973), 415 ff.

5. In England 'reparation' includes both 'restitution' and 'compensation'. Restitution in legal terminology means the return of the actual property which has been removed; and that is what a restitution order enjoins. Compensation means the giving of something else, usually money; and that is what a compensation order enjoins. But in both the UK and the USA 'reparation' has come to be used to mean 'compensation'.

6. Only the Netherlands' scheme seems not to insist on his co-operation. See the Council of Europe's *Research on Victimisation*, Strasbourg, 1985.

7. See D. Hodgson (chairman), *The Profits of Crime and their Recovery: Report of a Committee*, London, Heinemann, 1984.

8. See J. M. Van Dijk, 'Regaining a Sense of Community and Order', in *Research on Victimisation*.

9. See T. Marshall and M. Walpole, *Bringing People Together: Mediation and Reparation Projects in Great Britain*, London, HMSO, 1985.

10. Mention should also be made of a few schemes which involve victims in meeting not the offenders from whom they personally have suffered but offenders guilty of similar offences. Victims of rape or violence from a stranger are too likely to be disturbed by meeting their own attacker.

Chapter 16: Preventing and Fighting

1. See P. Mayhew *et al.*, *Crime as Opportunity*, London, HMSO, 1976; J. M. Chaiken *et al.*, *Impact of Police Activities on Crime: Robberies on the New York City Subway System*, Santa Monica, Rand, 1974.

2. See T. H. Bennett and R. Wright, *Burglars on Burglary*, London, Heinemann, 1984.

3. The introduction of credit cards, incidentally, did not mean that less money was misappropriated. It is even possible that more was. The gains and losses, however, were transferred to different sorts of people. Any teenager can steal a wallet or a handbag, but it takes an experienced adult to handle a stolen credit card. As for the losses, some of these are borne by the companies which provide credit cards.

4. The Home Secretary's White Paper of 1964 took up the slogan, and was called *The War Against Crime in England and Wales 1959–1964*

(Cmnd. 2296., London, HMSO, 1964). Its contents were about as warlike as a drill manual.

5. The term used by Mathiesen to describe Norwegian prisoners' way of discrediting staff by pointing out their failures to follow the rules of the establishment. According to Bukovsky it works even in the USSR. See T. Mathiesen, *The Defences of the Weak*, London, Tavistock, 1965, and V. Bukovsky, *To Build a Castle*, tr. M. Scammell, New York, Penguin, Viking, 1978.

6. For an excellent discussion of this topic, see Glanville Williams's *The Proof of Guilt*, 1963 edition, London, Stevens.

7. See the *Eleventh Report of the Criminal Law Revision Committee: Evidence* (General), Cmnd. 4991, London, HMSO, 1972.

Chapter 17: Politics and Criminology

1. See the 1986 edition of *The Sentence of the Court*, London, HMSO, which ignores the findings of professional follow-ups, and simply says that 80 per cent of probation orders are successfully completed. Successful completion depends on the efficiency and tolerance of the probation officer.

2. A finding of one of the Home Office surveys described in *Sentencing and the Public*, N. Walker and M. Hough (edd.), Aldershot, Gower, 1987.

3. A. Medea and K. Thompson, *Against Rape*, London, Peter Owen, 1975.

Further Reading

Laws and Rules

S. Roberts, *Order and Dispute: an Introduction to Legal Anthropology*, Harmondsworth, Penguin, 1979.

J. Raz, *Practical Reason and Norms*, London, Hutchinson, 1975.

H. L. A. Hart, *The Concept of Law*, London, Oxford University Press, 1961.

Fictions and Figures

K. A. Bottomley and C. A. Coleman, *Understanding Crime Rates*, Farnborough, Gower, 1981.

Natural History

S. Hurwitz and K. O. Christiansen, *Criminology*, London, Allen and Unwin, 1983.

Behaviour and Misbehaviour

N. Walker, *Behaviour and Misbehaviour: Explanations and Non-Explanations*, Oxford, Blackwell, 1975.

Rule-Breaking and Rationality

R. Harré and P. F. Secord, *The Explanation of Social Behaviour*, Oxford, Blackwell, 1972.

D. B. Cornish and R. V. Clarke (edd.), *The Reasoning Criminal: Rational Choice Perspectives on Offending*, New York, Berlin, Springer-Verlag, 1986.

Sentencing and Not Sentencing

N. Walker, *Sentencing: Theory, Law and Practice*, London, Butterworths, 1985.

Sentences and Justifications

N. Walker, *Sentencing: Theory, Law and Practice*, London, Butterworths, 1985, Chapter 6.

Deterrence and Education

J. Gibbs, *Crime, Punishment and Deterrence*, Amsterdam, Elsevier, 1975.

G. Hawkins and F. Zimring, *Deterrence: the legal threat in crime control*, Chicago, University of Chicago Press, 1973.

Incapacitation and Dangerousness

J. E. Floud and W. Young, *Dangerousness and Criminal Justice*, London, Heinemann, 1981.

J. B. Coker and J. P. Martin, *Licensed to Live*, Oxford, Blackwell, 1985.

Desert and Ritual

P. Bean, *Punishment: a philosophical and criminological inquiry*, Oxford, Martin Robertson, 1981.

W. Moberly, *The Ethics of Punishment*, London, Faber and Faber, 1968.

Juveniles and Justice

H. Giller and A. Morris, *Understanding Juvenile Justice*, London, Croom Helm, 1987.

H. Parker, *View From The Boys*, Newton Abbott, David and Charles, 1974.

D. J. West, *Delinquency: Its Roots, Careers and Prospects*, London, Heinemann, 1982.

Anonymity and Stigma

E. Goffman, *Stigma: Notes on the Management of Spoiled Indentity*, Harmondsworth, Penguin, 1968.

Criminalizing and Decriminalizing

H. L. A. Hart, *The Morality of the Criminal Law: Two Essays*, London, Oxford University Press, 1965.

H. L. Packer, *The Limits of the Criminal Sanction*, California, Stanford University Press, 1969.

B. Mitchell, *Law, Morality and Religion in a Secular Society*, London, Oxford University Press, 1970.

Victims and Victimology

I. Drapkin and E. Viano, *Victimology: a New Focus*, Lexington, Heath, 1974.

Preventing and Fighting

G. Laycock and K. Heal (edd.), *Situational Crime Prevention: From Theory into Practice*, London, HMSO 1986.

Politics and Criminology

P. Norton (ed.), *Law and Order and British Politics*, Aldershot, Gower, 1984.

Index

OXFORD

MORE OXFORD PAPERBACKS

Details of a selection of other books follow. A complete list of Oxford Paperbacks, including The World's Classics, Twentieth-Century Classics, OPUS, Past Masters, Oxford Authors, Oxford Shakespeare, and Oxford Paperback Reference, is available in the UK from the General Publicity Department, Oxford University Press (JH), Walton Street, Oxford OX2 6DP.

In the USA, complete lists are available from the Paperbacks Marketing Manager, Oxford University Press, 200 Madison Avenue, New York, NY 10016.

Oxford Paperbacks are available from all good bookshops. In case of difficulty, customers in the UK can order direct from Oxford University Press Bookshop, 116 High Street, Oxford, Freepost, OX1 4BR, enclosing full payment. Please add 10 per cent of published price for postage and packing.

PRISONS AND THE PROCESS OF JUSTICE

Andrew Rutherford

In this book Andrew Rutherford, a leading commentator on judicial matters and an outspoken critic of contemporary British penal policy, surveys the full criminal justice process; compares policies of prosecution, sentencing, and imprisonment internationally; and argues powerfully for a radical reduction in the number of people in prison.

'a book which combines academic rigour with prophetic vision . . . This is a book that deserves to be read widely and, above all, used as a springboard for action. It could prove to be one of the most important books of the decade.' *Crucible*

'*Prisons and the Process of Justice* is a marvellous polemic. At a time of immovable expansion, it has an irresistible force.' *London Review of Books*

CHANGE IN BRITISH SOCIETY 3/e

A. H. Halsey

This book was first published in 1978 as an expanded version of that year's Reith Lectures; it has been continually updated, and the third edition constitutes a substantial revision of the original, with the inclusion of important new material. The author is a distinguished sociologist who here analyses the direction British society has taken in this century. He points to changes involving class and status, social and geographical mobility, standards of living and family, and explains how these changes have been affected by patterns of economic growth, liberal and Marxist political theories, and the power of the State. An additional chapter is devoted to changes in the accessibility, ideals, and practice of education.

This lucidly argued, honest book offers a provocative analysis of British society. It raises questions of importance to us all and proposes solutions which are at once sane and radical.

UNHOLY PLEASURE:

The Idea of Social Class

P. N. Furbank

'People in Britain at the moment talk too much about "class"', writes P. N. Furbank in his fascinating study of this particularly British social phenomenon. He explores the derivation of our ideas about social status, and our intentions in deploying 'class' terminology, and concludes that the concept of class has really had its day.

'This elegant and witty book is the retort of a literary critic and biographer to the pretensions of the social sciences.' *Observer*

'draws attention to the many confusions surrounding the word "class" . . . entertaining and stimulating.' *British Book News*

LAW AND MORALS

Warnock, Gillick, and Beyond

Simon Lee

This highly topical book examines the relationship between law and morals, and relates its findings to such issues of current debate as discrimination, abortion, contraception for teenagers, experiments on embryos, and surrogate motherhood. It exposes popular misconceptions, and asks us to go beyond outdated ethical arguments to a new realization that by separating our moral from our factual disagreements, society may yet come to a consensus on some of its most intractable questions.

'The outstanding virtue of this book is the brevity with which it deals with such a substantial list of subjects. Nobody can pretend to find it too long or too difficult, though it does make demands and stimulate questions. Even for those who disagree with its conclusions, it is important.'
Catholic Herald

'a marvellous book' *New Society*

'This is an excellent and thought-provoking book.' *Universe*

LAW AND MODERN SOCIETY
P. S. Atiyah

'The Oxford University Press has done well to publish this brief, lucid and stimulating appraisal by P. S. Atiyah of English law as it operates in our society today. And it is refreshing to find that Professor Atiyah describes the law in action before he asks his questions. His study is critical, but not damning. Though Atiyah is careful not to state his own position and sensibly emphasizes that without judges educated by training and experience to handle and develop constitutional safeguards a Bill of Rights is unlikely to achieve its purpose, I find the conclusion to be drawn from his reasoning inescapable. It points to the need for constitutional reform. Atiyah leaves it to his readers to decide what they want. It is good, therefore, that the book is designed to be read by all who are interested; that it is written in a style which all can appreciate; that it is brief; and that it is modestly priced.' Leslie Scarman, *Times Literary Supplement*

'The author surveys the legal system rather than substantive law and has views on judges, the legal profession generally, the way lawyers themselves regard law, law and the state and "Bad law" Throughout the text he tries to be fair where there are two political viewpoints . . . the book is a stimulating introduction to the legal system for the intelligent layman.' *Solicitors Journal*

An OPUS book

MARX'S SOCIAL THEORY
Terrell Carver

Why has Marx had such a wide-ranging impact on our intellectual and political life? Terrell Carver presents a new analysis of what Marx called the 'guiding thread' of his studies, which is set out in his 1859 preface *A Critique of Political Economy*, together with an important autobiographical sketch, which the author reanalyses in this book. He argues that Marx's 'production theory of society and social change' is analogous to Darwin's work in a hitherto unnoticed way and is just as scientific. He assesses the central difficulties encountered by the theory, and shows that it sprang from a desire not simply to interpret the world, but to change it.